# Credits

Recipes by:                                  Beatrice Youil
Recipe Translator:                        Rima Youil
Recipe Testers:                            Rita Youil, Rima Youil
Photography and Cover Art:           Rowland Youil
Writing, Typesetting and Editing: Rowland Youil

Published by Nabu Books Ltd
www.nabubooks.com

ISBN 978-0957589209

# Contents

## Rice 75

## Mains 97

# Notes

* All measurements of spoon and cups are levelled quantities. Plain flour is used in all recipes that require it, unless otherwise stated.

* When measuring fresh herbs, dice first and lightly pack into the measuring cup or spoon.

* Metric and imperial measures for temperature (Centigrade/Fahrenheit) and weight (gram/oz) are noted in this book. The conversions are rounded for convenience.

* The recipes in this book are very forgiving, so adding a little more or less meat, herb or vegetable will not affect the overall taste of the dish.

## Measuring utensils used

| Measure | Qty |
|---|---|
| 1 cup | 250 ml |
| ½ cup | 125 ml |
| 1 Tbsp (Tablespoon) | 15 ml |
| 1 tsp (teaspoon) | 5 ml |

## Oven temperatures

| Centigrade | Fahrenheit | Gas Mark |
|---|---|---|
| 150 °C | 300 °F | Gas 2 |
| 160 °C | 325 °F | Gas 3 |
| 180 °C | 350 °F | Gas 4 |
| 200 °C | 400 °F | Gas 6 |
| 220 °C | 425 °F | Gas 7 |
| 240 °C | 475 °F | Gas 9 |

# Using this book

Each recipe has a small information box that gives the approximate preparation time, cooking time, servings and caloric information. The preparation time may also contain any soaking that may be necessary for the recipe (e.g. soak chickpeas in water overnight). The cooking time will also include any refrigeration or freezing that may be required before serving. It is recommended that before you begin a recipe, check if there is any pre-preparation needed.

The caloric information is a rough estimate and should only be used as a very general guide to the calorie content of the food per serving.

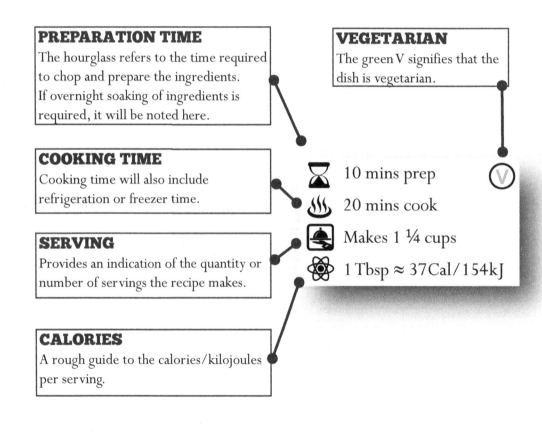

**PREPARATION TIME**
The hourglass refers to the time required to chop and prepare the ingredients.
If overnight soaking of ingredients is required, it will be noted here.

**COOKING TIME**
Cooking time will also include refrigeration or freezer time.

**SERVING**
Provides an indication of the quantity or number of servings the recipe makes.

**CALORIES**
A rough guide to the calories/kilojoules per serving.

**VEGETARIAN**
The green V signifies that the dish is vegetarian.

10 mins prep
20 mins cook
Makes 1 ¼ cups
1 Tbsp ≈ 37Cal/154kJ

# Acknowledgements

A special thanks to the following companies for the kind loan of accessories for the photography.

**Spode** is a British company founded by Josiah Spode I in 1770 in the town of Stoke-on-Trent in the UK. Their stunning signature "Blue Italian" pieces can be seen on pages 143, 151. www.spode.co.uk

**Aynsley** is a British company founded in 1775 that produces fine china pieces. Their beautiful black and white "Mozart" design plateware can be seen on pages 53, 85, 87, 138. www.aynsley.co.uk

**KitchenAid** is an American kitchen appliance company that first created the stand mixer in 1919. Their retro Artisan mixer (pictured left) was used for making the bread and pastries in this book. It can be seen on pages 129, 134. www.kitchenaid.com

# Introduction

An Assyrian kitchen is a busy place. There is always something cooking: a pot on the stove, food baking in the oven, or tea brewing for the unexpected guest. This book is about the food prepared in our mum's kitchen. Some of the recipes are well know Middle Eastern dishes but most will be new to you.

Assyria was an ancient civilisation from the Mesopotamian region dating back thousands of years. The country no longer exists but Assyrians can be found almost anywhere in the world.

Like many other cultures, recipes take on regional influences. My mum was born in Iran, so the recipes have a Persian influence. Lamb stews, stuffed vine leaves and hearty soups are popular dishes. Chickpeas, beans, fresh herbs and basmati rice are all mainstay ingredients.

There are some national dishes that most Assyrians like to prepare such as Booshala (yoghurt soup), Chipteh (meatball and bulgur wheat stew), Dolma (rice stuffed vine leaves and vegetables) and Harrissa (wheat porridge).

Almost all the ingredients used in this book are readily available from the supermarket. A very small number are not as common but don't despair as alternatives can be used as outlined in the last chapter titled "The pantry" on page 155.

The initial purpose for writing this book was to document the recipes for our own enjoyment but we are pleased to be able to share them with you.

A special thanks to our mum, Beatrice, for being such a wonderful cook.

-Rowland

# Mezze

A selection of appetisers, snacks and breakfast dishes

# red onion sauce
## ❧booleh gilya❧

1 large brown onion (diced)
⅓ cup vegetable oil
3 cloves garlic (finely diced)
2 Tbsp tomato paste
1 Tbsp sweet paprika powder
½ tsp black pepper
¼ tsp salt

 10 mins prep  (V)
20 mins cook
Makes 1 ¼ cups
 1 Tbsp ≈ 37 Cal / 154 kJ

*Many Assyrian dishes use onions, paprika, pepper and tomato paste as their base.*

*Ensure you have a good supply of these ingredients in your pantry.*

*A mild or hot paprika can be used in this recipe for an extra kick.*

1. Heat the oil in a pan and add the onion and salt. Sauté for about 7 - 8 minutes on medium heat until onions begin to lightly brown and caramelise. Mix occasionally to ensure onions lightly brown evenly.
2. Stir in the garlic, tomato paste, pepper and paprika and fry for a further 2 minutes. The oil should be a bright orange / red.
3. Slowly add ½ cup of water to make a thick sauce and simmer for a further 2 mins on a low heat.

This sauce is eaten warm. Drizzle over dolma or fried eggplant or use as a condiment.

# yoghurt and cucumber
## ❧mustah khiare❧

2 cups of full cream natural or Greek style yoghurt
1 garden variety cucumber
½ cup chopped fresh dill
½ tsp salt

 10 mins prep  (V)
No cooking
Makes 2¼ cups
 1 Tbsp ≈ 10 Cal / 42 kJ

*This refreshing combination of yoghurt, cucumber and dill is great with spicy food or as a dip.*

1. Deseed and dice the cucumbers.
2. In a bowl add the yoghurt, dill and diced cucumber.
3. Mix well and add salt to taste.

Use as a dip or as a side dish with a main meal.

# yoghurt garlic sauce
## ❧mustah toomah❧

2 cups of full cream natural yoghurt
1 garlic clove crushed
½ tsp salt

 5 mins prep  (V)
 No cooking
 Makes 2 cups
1 Tbsp ≈ 10 Cal / 42 kJ

*This versatile sauce can be used as a dressing for fried eggplant, zucchini, vine leaf dolma and as a sandwich condiment.*

1. In a bowl simply add the yoghurt and crushed garlic.
2. Mix well adding salt to taste.

Use as a dip, as a salad dressing or in a kebab wrap. Use an extra clove of garlic for a stronger taste.

# chickpea dip
## ⮞hummus⮜

420g(15oz) can chickpeas
2 Tbsp tahini (sesame paste)
2 Tbsp of olive oil
2 Tbsp lemon juice
¼ tsp grated lemon zest
1 clove garlic crushed
Optional: ¼ tsp grated lemon zest
¼ tsp salt
Sweet paprika and extra olive oil for garnish

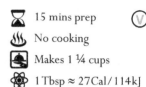

15 mins prep
No cooking
Makes 1 ¼ cups
1 Tbsp ≈ 27Cal / 114kJ

1. Drain the can of chickpeas, reserving the liquid.
2. In a blender or food processor, combine chickpeas, tahini, garlic, lemon juice, lemon zest, olive oil, ¼ cup reserved liquid and salt until a smooth paste is formed. Taste and add extra salt if required.
3. If the mixture is too thick add some extra reserved chickpea liquid and blend.

Pour the hummus into a serving bowl. Drizzle with olive oil and dust with sweet paprika. Serve with oven toasted pita bread (below), crackers or your favourite crisps.

*Crispy pita provides a perfect dip companion.*

# oven toasted pita

Pita bread
Olive oil

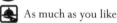
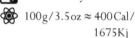

10 mins prep
15 mins cook
As much as you like
100g / 3.5oz ≈ 400Cal / 1675Kj

1. Preheat oven to 170°C/340°F
2. Split pita bread and brush both sides with olive oil.
3. Cut into wedges. Use as much pita as you need.
4. Spread the cut pita bread out on the baking tray and bake for 10-15 minutes until crisp and golden.
5. Remove from oven and leave to cool in the tray.

*This is another middle eastern favourite that is easy to make.*

*For an extra tasty smoky flavour, roast the eggplants on a barbecue.*

# eggplant dip
## ❧baba ghanoush❧

3 medium eggplants (750g/1½ lb)
1 Tbsp tahini
4 Tbsp lemon juice
2 Tbsp olive oil
2 clove of garlic (unpeeled)
½ tsp sweet paprika
½ tsp salt

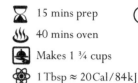

15 mins prep
40 mins oven
Makes 1 ¾ cups
1 Tbsp ≈ 20 Cal/84kJ

1. Heat oven to 200°C/400°F
2. Place whole eggplants on an aluminium lined baking tray and cook in the oven for 40 minutes. Half way through the cooking process, turn the eggplants over and add the unpeeled garlic to the tray.
3. Remove from oven and leave to cool.
4. Cut eggplants in half and scoop out the flesh. Roughly chop. You may want to remove some of the excess liquid from the eggplant by placing in a sieve over a sink and gently press with the back of a spoon (this is an optional step).
5. In a bowl add the chopped eggplant, tahini, lemon juice, olive oil, paprika, roasted garlic (peeled and crushed) and salt.
6. Beat together with a wooden spoon to break apart the eggplant and mix all the ingredients together. You can use a food processor but do not over mix, it should retain some texture.
7. Add extra salt if needed.

Pour into a dip bowl, drizzle with a little olive oil and it's ready to serve. Try with fresh pita bread, oven toasted pita (page 16) or any of your favourite crackers or crisps.

# fried eggplant and zucchini
## ❧bodemjon-eh chuma va gorreh❧

2 large eggplants 500g (1 lb)
2 large zucchini 500g (1 lb)
½ portion of garlic yoghurt (page 14)
½ portion of red onion sauce (page 14)
Vegetable Oil for frying
Salt

⧗ 1 hr. 10 mins prep  Ⓥ
♨ 20 mins frying
🔔 6 servings
⚛ 1 srv ≈ 270 Cal / 1130 kJ
*(not including dressing)*

*The eggplant needs to be salted to draw out the bitterness and excess water. This will also prevent the eggplant from absorbing too much oil when frying.*

## Prepare eggplant

1. Peel the eggplants and slice to ½ cm (¼″) thickness lengthwise. Place in a colander over a sink and sprinkle liberally with salt.
2. Leave for 1 hour for the eggplant to release water.
3. Take each piece of eggplant and wipe down with a clean tea towel or absorbent kitchen paper to remove the leached water and salt.

## Prepare zucchini

4. You do not need to peel the zucchini but you can if you prefer. Remove the tops and slice to ½ cm (¼″) thickness lengthwise. Do not add salt.

## Cooking

5. In a pan, add enough vegetable oil to cover the base. Add two or three slices of eggplants at a time and shallow fry to give a golden brown colour. Turn over to brown the other side. The pan will require topping up with oil every now and again.
6. Place the fried eggplant on a flat plate that has been lined with absorbent kitchen paper to drain the excess oil. Continue until all the eggplant has been fried.
7. Repeat the cooking process with the zucchini.

Serve warm with a dollop of garlic yoghurt and red onion sauce. This dish is usually part of a buffet of food placed in the center of the table and served family style.

# omelette with yoghurt
## ❧joozllama❧

*An egg omelette with garlic yoghurt may seem a strange combination, but it works.*

*This is delicious for breakfast or as a quick snack.*

4 large eggs
1 Tbsp flour
¼ tsp of salt
Pinch of pepper
¼ cup vegetable oil
¼ portion of the yoghurt garlic sauce (page 14)

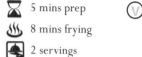

5 mins prep
8 mins frying
2 servings
1 srv ≈ 400 Cal/1674 kJ

1. Heat the vegetable oil on a medium/high heat in a heavy based pan (size: 26 cm/10″). The oil should cover the base of the pan.
2. Crack the eggs in a bowl. Add the flour, salt and pepper, and beat using a fork until blended. Don't worry about any lumps.
3. Pour the egg mixture into the heated oil and allow it to bubble. Slide a spoon under the omelette and lift it slightly to allow the uncooked egg to flow underneath. Do this until the omelette begins to set.
4. When golden brown underneath, flip the omelette over and brown the other side. It may be easier to cut omelette into quarters and flip each of those. When browned underneath it is ready to serve.

Spoon over the yoghurt garlic sauce and serve immediately.
Eat as is or with bread.

# omelette with honey
## ∽spirra∽

4 large eggs
1 Tbsp flour
¼ tsp ground black pepper
¼ tsp of salt
¼ cup vegetable oil
¼ cup honey

5 mins prep
8 mins frying
2 servings
1 srv ≈ 487Cal / 2039kJ

(V)

*This is delicious for breakfast or as a quick snack.*

1. Make the omelette as per the previous omelette recipe (page 22).
2. Take off the heat and instead of the yoghurt, drizzle with honey.
3. Serve immediately.

Eat as is or with bread.

# eggs and tomato
## ❧beeyeh bodemjon❧

4 large eggs
2 Tbsp butter
3 medium ripe tomatoes
Salt and pepper to taste
Optional: a small mild green pepper or sweet Romano pepper

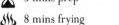 5 mins prep
 8 mins frying
2 servings
 1 srv ≈ 307Cal/1285kJ

Ⓥ

*Another breakfast treat. This is delicious with crusty bread.*

1. Melt the butter in a heavy pan.
2. Roughly chop the tomatoes and add to pan. If using the green pepper, thinly slice and add to the pan as well.
3. Season with the salt and crushed pepper.
4. Gently cook the tomatoes on medium heat. Put the lid on the pan to allow the tomatoes to soften. This will take about 5 minutes.
5. Crack the eggs over the tomatoes in the pan.
6. Cover pan with lid for a minute or two. Take care not to overcook the eggs. The yolks should remain runny.

Serve with buttered toast or crusty bread.

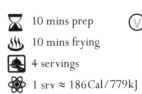

10 mins prep  (V)

10 mins frying

4 servings

1 srv ≈ 186 Cal / 779 kJ

*This herb omelette is often used as a side dish for a main meal.*

*Use only fresh herbs for this recipe.*

# herb omelette
## ❧spira gelaleh(khookhoo)❧

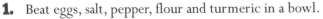

4 large eggs
¼ cup of finely chopped dill
¼ cup of finely chopped coriander
¼ cup of finely chopped parsley
¼ cup of finely chopped spring onions
½ tsp turmeric
1 Tbsp flour
¼ tsp ground black pepper
¼ tsp salt
¼ cup of vegetable oil

1. Beat eggs, salt, pepper, flour and turmeric in a bowl.
2. Add the chopped dill, coriander, parsley and spring onions to the egg mixture. Mix well.
3. Heat the oil in a heavy based pan (size: 26 cm / 10″) on medium heat. Pour the herb mixture into the hot oil.
4. Once the herb omelette has started to set, lift the side to check that it has started to brown. Flip over to brown the other side.

To serve, cut into wedges. This can be eaten for breakfast, but is often served as a side dish or part of a buffet.

# cream cheese with herbs
### ⤖djadjoodge⤖

300g(10½oz) tub of cottage, ricotta
    or Philadelphia cheese
3 spring onions
5 leaves of fresh basil
1 green chilli pepper (mild)
Optional: 1 Tbsp of finely chopped fresh oregano
Salt and black pepper to taste

⌛ 10 mins prep
♨ No cooking
🍵 Makes 1½ cups
⚛ 1 Tbsp ≈ 26 Cal / 108 kJ
Ⓥ

*This can be eaten for breakfast with fresh bread and sweet tea.*

*It also makes a tasty addition to a cheese platter.*

1. Finely dice the spring onions, chilli pepper, basil and oregano.
2. Add the chopped herbs and chilli to the soft cheese and mix well.
3. Season with salt and pepper to taste.

This cheese can be served like a dip or used in canapés.


# garlic walnut pesto
### ⤖jawzeh va touma⤖

100g(3½oz) shelled walnuts
2 cloves of garlic (crushed)
1 cup of chopped parsley
¼ cup of vegetable oil
½ tsp salt

⌛ 10 mins prep
♨ No cooking
🍵 Makes 1 cup
⚛ 1 Tbsp ≈ 68 Cal / 287 kJ
Ⓥ

*When we were children, we used to eat this spread over soft white sliced bread.*

1. Add all the ingredients into a food processor.
2. Use the pulse setting to quickly mix the ingredients being careful not to over blend. There should still be texture to the walnuts. Occasionally wipe down the sides of the bowl to ensure it is mixed evenly.

This pesto can be used as a sandwich spread. It can also be used as a base for pasta or stuffing under the skin of roast chicken (see page 122).

# cumin cheese
## ❧djoopta dmertah❧

200g Pecorino cheese
2 tsp whole caraway seeds or cumin seeds

Overnight soaking  Ⓥ
No cooking
Makes 200g
1 Tbsp ≈ 50 Cal / 209 kJ

1. Place the caraway or cumin seeds in a small glass with ¼ cup of water. Leave to soak overnight.
2. Grate the Pecorino cheese and add 3 Tbsp of water. Add the drained seeds and mix through.
3. Press the cheese mixture into a ceramic or glass container. Ensure you press it down firmly so that the cheese reforms into a hard block.
4. While it can be eaten immediately, it is best to leave this covered in the fridge for up to 5 days to let the cumin flavour infuse into the cheese.

Serve on crackers or with bread.

# brown easter eggs

**6 eggs**
**2 large handfuls of brown onion skin**

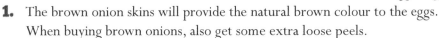

⏳ 5 mins prep

🔥 15 minutes

🍳 Makes 6 eggs

⚛ 1 egg ≈ 70Cal / 293kJ

Ⓥ

*These eggs are traditionally eaten during Easter.*

*A game is usually played where everyone chooses an egg and then attempts to crack the tip of each other's egg. The person whose egg remains intact is the winner.*

1. The brown onion skins will provide the natural brown colour to the eggs. When buying brown onions, also get some extra loose peels.
2. In a stainless steel pot add a handful of the brown onion skins.
3. Lay the eggs carefully over the onion skins and pour cold water to cover the eggs.
4. Add the rest of the onion skins over the top.
5. Bring to the boil and simmer for 15 minutes. The water will become a dark brown.
6. Take off the heat and let the eggs remain in the water for another 15 minutes.
7. Remove the eggs and arrange in a basket.

You can also create patterns by wrapping thread around the egg before boiling.

# piroshki

### DOUGH
1 Tbsp dry yeast
1½ cups milk (warm)
2 eggs (lightly beaten)
1 tsp sugar
4 cups flour
1 tsp sodium bicarbonate
1 tsp salt
2 Tbsp vegetable oil
2 Tbsp yoghurt

### GLAZE (OVEN BAKING)
1 egg
1 Tbsp Yoghurt

### FILLING
250g (9oz) minced meat
3 Tbsp vegetable oil
1 medium onion diced
1 large potato
4 eggs (hard boiled)
1 Tbsp curry powder
½ tsp pepper
½ tsp paprika
½ tsp salt

Optional: Oil for deep
frying

1 ½ hrs prep
20 mins oven
Makes 20 patties
1 patty ≈ 195 Cal / 816 kJ
(Oven baked)

## Dough
1. Mix the yeast and sugar with warm milk in a large mixing bowl. Stir in 1 Tbsp flour and leave for 10 minutes in a warm place to activate the yeast. Stir in the yoghurt, oil and eggs.
2. To this yeast mixture, stir in the sifted flour, salt and sodium bicarbonate to form a soft dough. Knead for 5 minutes until smooth and elastic.
3. Drizzle with a little oil and cover with plastic wrap and leave in a warm place for an hour. The dough will double in size.

## Filling
4. Sauté the diced onions in a large pan with 3 Tbsp oil until just beginning to brown. Add the minced meat and fry for about 6-8 minutes until the meat is cooked.
5. Stir in the curry, pepper, paprika and salt and cook for a minute.
6. Chop the potato into small ½ cm (¼″) cubes and add to the meat.
7. Add ¼ cup of water and cook for 10 minutes until the potato starts to soften.
8. In a separate plate, mash the hard boiled eggs with the back of a fork to form pea sized pieces. Add to the rest of the filling.
9. Take off heat and leave to cool to room temperature before using.

## Assembling the piroshki
10. Preheat the oven to 200°C (400 °F)
11. Knock back the dough and divide into 2 balls. Roll each out to a thin pizza base thickness. Cut out 12 cm (5″) diameter disks. Add 1-2 tablespoons of the filling and fold over. Pinch the ends together to prevent filling from falling out. They should resemble a half moon.
12. Arrange on a lined baking tray. Leave to rest for 15 mins.

## Cooking (Either bake in the oven or deep fry)
13. **Oven baking**: Gently brush each piroshki with the glaze made by beating the egg and yoghurt. Bake in oven for 8-12 minutes until golden brown.
14. **Deep frying:** Add oil to the deep fryer and heat to 180°C (350°F). Gently place the piroshki in the fryer, turning over periodically for a few minutes until golden brown. Place cooked piroshki on kitchen paper to drain.

Serve warm from the oven or from the fryer. These will keep for a day or two in the fridge and can be reheated in the microwave or oven, but I doubt they will last that long.

# assyrian hamburgers
## ✂cutleteh✂

*They are hard to
resist and taste
great even when
eaten with nothing
more than a
dollop of tomato
sauce (ketchup).*

30 mins prep

20 mins frying

Makes 16 patties

1 patty ≈ 140Cal/583kJ

500g (1 lb) minced beef (or lamb)
1 medium brown onion
1 medium potato
1 large egg
¼ cup bread crumbs
1 tsp paprika
1 tsp ground black pepper
1 tsp salt


Extra bread crumbs for coating
Vegetable Oil for shallow pan frying

## Making the hamburger mix

1. Peel and finely grate the potato and onion.
2. In a large bowl add the minced meat, grated onion and potato along with any juices, the raw egg, ¼ cup bread crumbs, salt, pepper and paprika.
3. Knead all ingredients together by hand until well blended.

## Shaping the burgers

4. On a flat plate add about 1 cup bread crumbs.
5. Take a golf-ball size of the meat mixture and roll in the bread crumbs.
6. Form into an oval shape and then flatten between your palms.
7. Once the meat has been shaped, coat in the bread crumbs again.
8. Pat the meat patties slightly to ensure the bread crumbs stick and dust off any excess.

## Frying

9. Heat the oil on medium heat in a fry pan. Add enough oil (about ½ cm/¼″ deep) for shallow frying.
10. Carefully place the crumbed patties into the hot pan.
11. Cook until the patties are golden brown. Turn over and cook the other side.
12. Remove from the pan and drain onto absorbent kitchen paper.

Eat as you would a burger in a bun with tomatoes, lettuce, pickles and tomato sauce (ketchup). These burgers are also great in a wrap or flatbread.

# chicken and egg salad
## ❧salade olivieh❧

*This recipe was taught to our dad by a chef in Iran.*

*To make this vegetarian, simply omit the chicken.*

*It is great as a sandwich or baguette filling.*

3 medium potatoes (750g/1.7 lb)
4 large eggs
250g (9oz) chicken breast fillet
140g (5oz) dill pickled cucumbers
½ cup garden peas
1 Tbsp capers (diced)
¼ cup cream
½ cup of mayonnaise (see recipe below)
½ tsp salt

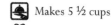

30 mins prep
20 mins cooking
Makes 5 ½ cups
½ cup ≈ 250Cal/1060kJ

### Preparation

1. Hard boil the eggs for 8-10 minutes. Set aside to cool.
2. Peel and then boil potatoes for about 15 minutes. Ensure that a fork enters smoothly, do not overcook. Set aside to cool.
3. Boil peas for 1 minute (frozen peas work well in this recipe).
4. Poach the chicken fillet in about 2 cm (1") of water in a pan for about 10- 15 minutes or until it has cooked through. Set aside to cool.

### Assemble the salad

5. Dice the potatoes and chicken into small cubes and add to a large bowl. Add the cooked peas, diced capers and diced dill pickles.
6. Mash the hard boiled eggs with the back of a fork . The pieces should be pea sized or smaller. Add to the bowl.
7. Add the cream and season with salt to taste. Carefully mix all the ingredients together.
8. Finally add the mayonnaise and gently stir through. Add extra salt if needed.

Plate the salad into a serving bowl. Use extra mayonnaise to spread a thin layer over the top of the salad. Decorate with olives. This is great as a side dish, sandwich filling or as a topping for canapés.

# mayonnaise

*The easiest way to make this is by using a small food processor or a hand mixer.*

*Use a quality vegetable oil.*

1 egg yolk (raw)
1 boiled egg (use yolk only)
2 tsp Dijon or Hot English mustard
2 Tbsp fresh lemon juice
1 cup vegetable oil (or half vegetable, half light olive oil)
¼ tsp salt

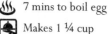

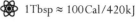

15 mins prep
7 mins to boil egg
Makes 1 ¼ cup
1 Tbsp ≈ 100Cal/420kJ

1. In a bowl add the raw egg yolk, finely grated hardboiled egg yolk, mustard, salt and 3 Tbsp of the oil.
2. Begin beating this until an emulsion forms. Gently start pouring the oil in a thin stream while continuously beating the mixture. The mayonnaise will begin to form.
3. Finally add the lemon juice and beat through.

# seafood dip

400g (14oz) Philadelphia cream cheese
1 can (160g/5.6oz) tuna (drained)
1 small can of shrimp or
        100g (3.5oz) cooked shrimp (diced)
1 tsp Tabasco sauce
1 Tbsp of lemon juice
1 Tbsp tomato sauce (ketchup)

10 mins prep

No cooking

Makes 600g (1.3 lb)

1 Tbsp ≈ 46 Cal/194 kJ

*Another of our
dad's recipes.*

*This is a delicious
dip that can
be used as a
sandwich spread
as well.*

1. Soften cheese in a bowl. Mix with a wooden spoon until it is smooth.
2. Add the tuna and mix well into the cheese.
3. Add the shrimp, Tabasco, lemon juice and ketchup, and mix together.
4. You don't need to add any salt as there should be enough in the tuna and the shrimp.
5. Serve in a dip bowl.

Great as a dip or as a sandwich spread.

It is important
to use a good
quality olive oil
for this recipe. The
flavour of the oil
adds to the dish.

# egg, tomato and cucumber salad

10 mins prep

7 mins cooking

Serves 4

1 srv ≈ 188 Cal/790 kJ

Ⓥ

**6 large eggs**
**1 medium tomato**
**Small cucumber (100g/3.5oz)**
**2 Tbsp extra virgin olive oil**
**¼ tsp salt**
**Sprinkle of freshly ground black pepper.**

1. Boil the eggs for 8-10 minutes so that they are hard boiled. Leave to cool.
2. Mash the hard boiled eggs using the back of a fork into small, evenly sized pieces.
3. Dice and deseed the tomato and cucumbers. Mix into the eggs.
4. Add the olive oil, salt and pepper. Using a fork mix all ingredients together.
5. Add additional salt if required.

This is great on crackers or as a sandwich filling.

# tabouleh salad

¼ cup bulgur cracked wheat
2 cups chopped parsley
¼ cup mint finely chopped
2 medium tomatoes diced
4 Tbsp Lemon juice
¼ cup olive oil
1 small mild chilli deseeded and finely chopped (optional)
¼ tsp salt

 15 mins prep/ 1 hour soaking
 No cooking
 Serves 6
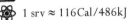 1 srv ≈ 116Cal/486kJ

Ⓥ

*Tabouleh is a healthy and fresh middle eastern salad popular in many countries.*

*You can substitute couscous in place of bulgur wheat. Use equal parts of couscous to hot water and let soak for about 5 minutes prior to adding to the tabouleh salad.*

1. Soak the bulgur wheat in 1 cup of boiling water and let sit for 1 hour.
2. Finely chop the mint, parsley, chilli and tomato, and add to a bowl.
3. Drain the bulgur wheat pressing out any excess water and add to the bowl containing the chopped herbs.
4. Add the lemon juice, salt and olive oil and mix thoroughly

This is a refreshing salad. It can also be used as an addition to sandwiches, hamburgers and wraps.

# garden salad

1 iceberg lettuce
1 small garden cucumber peeled and sliced
3 medium tomatoes
1 small capsicum
½ red onion
¼ cup mint finely chopped
¼ cup roughly chopped parsley
3 Tbsp lemon juice
2 Tbsp olive oil
salt and pepper to taste

⧗ 10 mins prep   Ⓥ
♨ no cooking
▦ Serves 6
⚛ 1 srv ≈ 120 Cal / 330 kJ

*A fresh garden salad is a great accompaniment to any meal.*

*You can also turn it into a quick lunch by just adding a pan fried piece of fish or chicken breast sliced over the top.*

1. Cut the iceberg lettuce into quarters and then slice into 2.5 cm (1″) chunks. Roughly separate the chunks by hand and add to a large salad bowl.
2. Cut the tomatoes into thick bite sized chunks. Add to the bowl.
3. Peel and thinly slice the red onion. Add to the bowl, along with the mint, parsley and sliced cucumbers.
4. Cut the capsicum in half and deseed. Thinly slice and add to the rest of the salad.
5. Sprinkle with salt and pepper and pour over the lemon juice and olive oil.
6. Toss the salad and make sure the vegetables are evenly distributed.

This garden salad can be eaten as a side to any main meal. Try it drizzled with sesame yoghurt sauce (recipe below).

# sesame yoghurt dressing

1 Tbsp tahini (sesame paste)
¼ cup natural full cream yoghurt
2 Tbsp lemon juice
1 tsp dijon mustard
salt
pepper

⧗ 5 mins prep   Ⓥ
♨ no cooking
▦ Serves 6
⚛ 1 srv ≈ 26 Cal / 110 kJ

1. In a small bowl mix together all the ingredients.
2. Add salt and pepper to taste.

Spoon this dressing over your favourite salad. Can also be used as a condiment for a kebab sandwich or hamburger.

*Instead of using
hard boiled eggs
you can add raw
beaten eggs to the
cooked spinach.
Continue cooking
and mix until the
eggs are cooked.*

# eggs and spinach
## ❧beeyeh spaun-ekh❧

500g(1 lb) Spinach (or silverbeet/chard)
4 eggs hard boiled
2 Tbsp butter
Salt

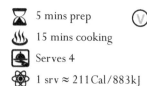

5 mins prep
15 mins cooking
Serves 4
1 srv ≈ 211 Cal/883 kJ

1. Hard boil the eggs (approx. 8-10 minutes in boiling water).
2. Wash spinach (or silverbeet) thoroughly.
3. Melt butter in a pot and add the spinach. Cover with lid.
4. Cook for 4 to 5 minutes on a low heat. The spinach will cook down and release water. Mix occasionally. Drain off any excess liquid.
5. Chop the boiled eggs into small pieces and mix through the spinach and serve.
6. Add salt to taste.

This is eaten at breakfast but can also be used as a side dish for main meals.

# chicken livers
## ᔕ•dje-djah-reh•ᔕ

500g (1 lb) chicken livers
1 large brown onion
50g (2oz) butter + 2 Tbsp vegetable oil
2 Tbsp tomato paste
1 tsp paprika
½ tsp ground black pepper
½ tsp salt

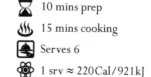

10 mins prep
15 mins cooking
Serves 6
1 srv ≈ 220Cal/921kJ

*When making this dish, try not to overcook the livers. They should be a little pink inside.*

*This also makes a great pâté spread. Add an extra 50g of butter when cooking. Once cooked, blend using a stick blender to form a smooth paste. Put into a resealable tub and refrigerate when cooled.*

1. Keep the livers in large pieces, removing any sinew.
2. Peel the onion and cut in half then slice thinly into half rings.
3. In a large pan melt the butter with the 2 Tbsp oil. Add the onions.
4. Sauté for about 6-8 minutes until the onions begin to lightly brown and caramelise. Mix occasionally to ensure onions brown evenly.
5. Stir in the paprika, salt and pepper and fry for a minute, then mix in the tomato paste.
6. Add the liver to the sauce and gently stir. Cook for about 5 minutes. Do not overcook.
7. Add 3 -4 Tbsp of water and mix in to create a sauce. Cook for a further minute.

This is eaten at breakfast on freshly buttered toast or with your favourite bread.

# Soups
**Tasty, healthy, hearty soups**

# beetroot soup
## ❧borscht❧

500g (1 lb) lamb shanks (approx. 2)
100g (3.5oz) cabbage
3 fresh beetroots (approx. 450g/1 lb)
2 medium carrots (approx. 150g/5oz)
3 medium potatoes (approx. 600g/1.3 lb)
400g (14oz) can of crushed tomatoes
3 bay leaves
½ tsp ground black pepper
1½ tsp salt
1 lemon
Bunch of parsley

30 mins prep

1½ hrs cooking

Serves 6

1 srv ≈ 310Cal/1290kJ

*Borscht originated in the Ukraine and is eaten all over the world.*

*As kids we always looked forward to when mum made this purple beetroot soup.*

*It is best served with a dollop of heavy or sour cream.*

1. Add the lamb shanks to a large pot with enough water to cover. Add salt and the bay leaves. Cover pot with lid slightly ajar (so that steam can escape).
2. Bring to the boil, then cook on medium/low heat for an hour.
3. Peel and chop the beetroots, carrots and potatoes into bite sized cubes. Slice and chop the cabbage into bite sized pieces.
4. After the lamb shanks have been cooking for an hour, add all these vegetables and the can of crushed tomatoes to the shanks. Add enough extra water to cover the vegetables.
5. Gently simmer for a further 30 mins until the cabbage and other vegetables have softened but still retain their shape. Add extra water if needed.
6. Squeeze the juice of the lemon directly into the pot. Taste and add extra salt and water if needed.
7. Just before serving, stir through a handful of roughly chopped parsley.

To serve, pull the meat from the lamb shank and portion out into each serving bowl. Ladle the borscht soup and vegetables over the meat. Add a dollop of fresh cream. Eat with fresh bread.

# chicken barley porridge
## ✥harrissa✥

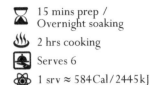
*This is eaten for breakfast or as a hearty winter lunch.*

*A quicker cooking alternative to barley is to use rolled oats. These will cook in less time and don't need soaking.*

1 whole medium chicken cut into pieces
2 cups pearl barley (soaked in water overnight)
2 tsp salt
Butter to serve
Cinnamon powder (optional)

## Soaking

1. In a bowl, add the 2 cups of pearl barley and enough water to cover.
2. Leave overnight to soak.

## Cooking

3. In a heavy bottomed pot bring 4 cups of water and the chicken pieces to the boil. Add the salt and simmer for 1 hour on medium/low heat. Cover with lid slightly ajar to allow the steam to escape.
4. Remove the chicken pieces from the broth and set aside.
5. Add the drained barley to the chicken broth and add an extra 3 cups of water and bring back to the boil. Reduce heat to medium/low and boil for 30 minutes, stirring occasionally.
6. Prepare the chicken by discarding the skin and pulling the meat from the bones. Tear the meat roughly into small pieces.
7. Add the boneless chicken pieces to the pot of barley and chicken stock and reduce heat to low. It is important to keep stirring so that the barley does not stick to the bottom off the pot and burn.
8. Cook for 30 more minutes, stirring regularly. The barley should be really soft to the bite. If not, add some more water (if it has become too thick) and keep cooking for 15 more minutes.
9. Add extra salt if required.

Serve hot. Pour into bowls and add a dollop of butter and a sprinkling of cinnamon powder.

# lamb and potato soup
## ❧shurve gordtorpe❧

500g (1 lb) boneless leg of lamb (cubed)
1 lamb leg joint bone
2 large onions (diced)
3 Tbsp vegetable oil + 1 Tbsp butter
3 medium potatoes
3 long green peppers or 1 large capsicum
2 Tbsp tomato paste
1 Tbsp paprika
1 tsp ground black pepper
1½ tsp salt

 20 mins prep

 1 hr cooking

Serves 6

1 srv ≈ 350Cal / 1460kJ

*Soups are eaten as main meals in Assyrian households.*

*Instead of croutons, fresh bread is torn into small pieces and dropped into the bowl to soak up the soup.*

1. In a large pot heat the oil and butter. Add the onions and salt and fry on medium heat until the onions soften (about 5 minutes).
2. Add the lamb and leg bone and stir through. Put the lid on the pot and cook for about 15 minutes. Keep an eye on the meat to ensure it doesn't burn, mixing occasionally. The cooking will draw out a lot of water from the meat.
3. Add black ground pepper, paprika, tomato paste and stir through.
4. Add 4 cups of water making sure to mix all the ingredients thoroughly to create a red soupy mix.
5. The long green peppers (or chopped capsicum) can now be added to the soup. Cover pot halfway with lid slightly ajar (so that steam can escape). Allow to cook on a medium low heat for 30 minutes.
6. Add another 2 cups of water.
7. Peel the potatoes and cut into halves or quarters so that they are still chunky. Add to the pot and simmer for another 20 minutes.
8. Check there is enough water to the soup. There should be enough soup for 6 bowls (including the potatoes). Add extra water if needed.
9. Add extra salt to taste.

Serve hot. Eat by dipping fresh bread into the soup and enjoy.

# chickpea and lamb soup
## ⊱aubagoosht⊰

500g (1 lb) lamb shanks (2 meaty shanks)
4 Tbsp vegetable oil
2 small onions
3 large tomatoes
6 small potatoes
½ cup chickpeas (soak overnight)
½ cup white beans (soak overnight)
1 tsp ground black pepper
2 tsp turmeric
½ tsp salt

⏳ 15 mins prep /
   overnight soaking

♨ 1½ hrs cooking

🍲 Serves 6

 1 srv ≈ 477Cal / 1997kJ

*Aubagoosht is a
well known Persian
and Assyrian dish.*

*Once cooked there
are two ways of
serving this dish :*

*1. Straight from the
pot to your bowl or*

*2. Remove the meat
and vegetables
from the soup
and mash them
together. Portion
this out into soup
bowls and pour the
soup over the top.*

*See picture on the
left for the serving
suggestions.*

## Soaking

**1.** Soak the chickpeas and white beans overnight in plenty of cold water.

## Cooking

**2.** Add 4 tablespoons of oil to a large pot and brown the lamb shanks for about 5 to 8 minutes. After browning, add 6 cups of water and bring to boil.

**3.** Skin the tomatoes by putting them in a heatproof bowl and pour over boiling water. Leave for a minute to loosen the skin. Carefully remove the tomatoes and peel. Cut into quarters.

**4.** Add the tomatoes, quartered onions, drained chickpeas and white beans to the pot with the lamb shanks. Simmer for 1 hour. Skim off any scum that may form on the surface of the broth while it is cooking.

**5.** Add the potatoes (peeled and cut in half), black pepper, turmeric and salt.

**6.** Cover pot halfway with lid slightly ajar and continue simmering for another 30 minutes (adding extra water if needed) or until the potatoes are fully cooked.

Pour stew into bowls ensuring each plate has beans, meat and potatoes. Eat with fresh bread.

Alternatively separate the meat, potatoes and beans from the soup. Mash roughly or to a smoother texture depending on your taste. In each plate add a dollop of the mashed mixture and pour the hot soup over it. Eat with fresh bread.

# lentil soup
## ᔥaddasᔥ

*You can use any variety of lentil for this recipe.*

*The large brown variety of lentils keep their shape and have a robust, rich flavour.*

 15 mins prep
 1 hr 10 mins cooking
 Serves 4
 1 srv ≈ 550Cal/2300kJ

2 cups brown lentils
2 Tbsp plain flour
1 portion of red onion sauce (page 14)
1 tsp salt

1. Prepare the red onion sauce as per page 14 and set aside.
2. Rinse lentils in cold water. In a large pot, add the drained lentils and 8 cups of water and bring to the boil.
3. Reduce heat and simmer for 40 minutes. Make sure the lentils are always covered by the water, adding extra when needed. Mix occasionally to prevent the lentils from sticking to the pot. The lid of the pot should be ajar to let steam escape.
4. Mix the flour and salt with ¼ cup water to form a smooth paste. Add this to the pot of lentils to thicken the soup.
5. Keep stirring for about 5 minutes otherwise the lentils will stick to the bottom of the pot.
6. Finally add the red onion sauce and mix through, cooking for a further 10 minutes on a low simmer. Keep mixing. This soup should be thick.

Serve in soup bowls with a dollop of sour cream or yoghurt.

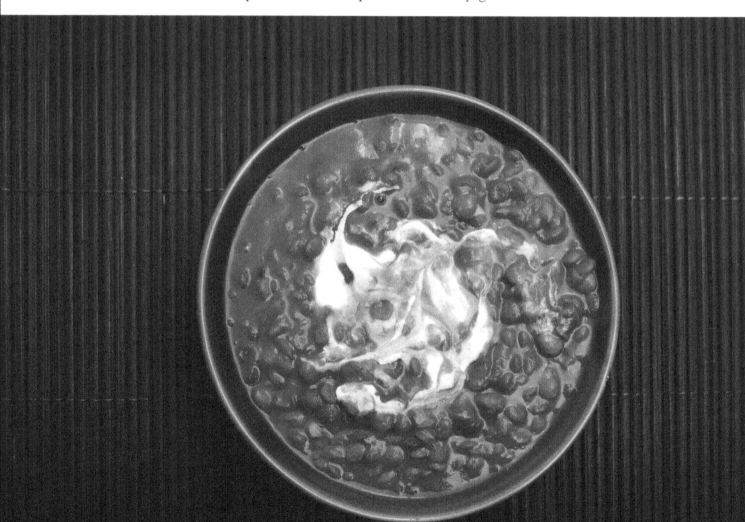

# red kidney beans
## ❧mahshe smooka❧

2 cups red kidney beans
2 Tbsp flour
1 portion of red onion sauce (page 14)
1 tsp salt

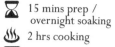 15 mins prep /
overnight soaking

 2 hrs cooking

Serves 4

1 srv ≈ 520 Cal / 2180 kJ

Ⓥ

*Beans are nutritious and make a filling lunch.*

*To save on cooking time you could cook the beans in a pressure cooker for 30 minutes following the cooker instructions rather than boil for an hour and half on a stove. The beans will be softer and have a better bite.*

1. Add the kidney beans to a large bowl. Cover with plenty of water and leave overnight on kitchen bench.
2. Make one portion of red onion sauce as per page 14. Set aside.
3. Drain beans and add to a large pot with 8 cups of water and simmer for 1½ hours on low heat. Ensure that the beans are covered with water during cooking. Add extra water when required. Mix occasionally to prevent any beans sticking to bottom of pot. The lid of the pot should be slightly ajar to let steam escape and prevent boiling over.
4. Mix the flour and salt with ¼ cup water to make a smooth paste. Add the flour paste to the pot of cooked beans and stir through.
5. Add the red onion sauce to the beans, stir through and cook for a further 10 minutes. Stir every few minutes to prevent the beans sticking to the bottom of the pot. The soup should be thick (not watery).

Serve in soup bowls with a dollop of sour cream or yoghurt.

61

# yoghurt and herb soup
## ⤖bushala⤖

1kg (2.2lb) natural full cream milk yoghurt
1 cup celery leaves (diced)
2 cups of flat parsley (diced)
2 cups of coriander (diced)
½ cup of fresh mint (diced)
3 cups of silverbeet/chard (diced)
1 cup of garlic chives (diced) (or use spring onions)
1 green capsicum (bell) or sweet romano pepper (cut into large pieces)
3 Tbsp flour
¼ cup short grain rice
1 large egg
2 tsp salt
Paprika for garnish and taste

⏳ 20 mins prep
♨ 20 mins cooking
🍲 Serves 6
⚛ 1 srv ≈ 220 Cal/925 kJ

Ⓥ

*This traditional Assyrian soup that can be served hot or cold.*

*Note that this recipe calls for celery leaves. This is the green leafy part of the celery. The stalk is not used in this recipe.*

1. Prepare all the herbs by washing thoroughly to remove any dirt. Remove the thick stalk from the silverbeet. Roughly dice all the greens, keeping the mint separate.
2. In a large pot, add the yoghurt, egg and rice and beat until smooth.
3. Next add 6 cups of cold water to the pot and stir gently.
4. Mix the flour with 1 cup of water and add to the pot.
5. Slowly bring to the boil on medium heat, continually stirring until the yoghurt soup starts bubbling. Add the bell pepper and mint.
6. Let boil for 15 minutes on medium/low heat stirring all the time. Add salt to taste.
7. Add the rest of the prepared herbs and mix through.
8. Continue gently stirring for the next 10 minutes.
9. Take off the heat and keep stirring for another 5 minutes.

Pour soup into bowls and sprinkle with a little sweet paprika. Leftovers can be refrigerated and served chilled.

# herb and bean noodle soup
## ❧aush-eh rishteh❧

⏳ 20 mins prep /
   overnight soaking Ⓥ

♨ 2 hrs cooking

🍲 Serves 6

⚛ 1 srv ≈ 485 Cal / 2031 kJ

*This vegetarian soup is filled with healthy herbs and is a popular Persian and Assyrian dish. It is important that you use fresh herbs for this recipe. However you could use 1 Tbsp dried oregano if you cannot find fresh.*

*There are many ingredients in this dish, so have them ready and chopped before beginning the cooking process.*

*This recipe is forgiving to changes so if you don't quite have enough of one herb, add extra of another.*

*To measure the herbs, dice first and lightly pack into the measuring cups.*

### SOUP
150g (5.3oz) dry tagliatelle egg noodles
2 cups parsley (diced)
2 cups coriander (diced)
2 cups silverbeet/chard (diced)
2 cups of garlic chives (diced)
    (or use spring onions)
½ cup chickpeas
½ cup white beans
½ cup red kidney beans
½ cup brown lentils
2 Tbsp flour
½ tsp salt

### RED SAUCE BASE
⅓ cup vegetable oil
1 medium brown onion (diced)
½ cup fresh mint (diced)
½ cup fresh oregano (diced)
3 cloves garlic (finely diced)
1 Tbsp tomato paste
1 Tbsp paprika
2 tsp turmeric
½ tsp black pepper
1 tsp salt

1. Soak the white beans, red beans and chickpeas overnight in a bowl with plenty of water.

**Prepare the herbs and greens**

2. In a large bowl mix together the finely diced parsley, coriander and garlic chives. Discard the thick stalk from the silverbeet and finely dice the green leaves and add to the bowl with the other herbs. Set aside. These will be added to the soup later.

3. Dice the oregano and mint and place in a separate bowl. These are for the red sauce.

**Red sauce base**

4. In a frying pan add ⅓ cup of oil and the diced onion. Sauté on medium heat for 7-8 minutes or until the onions begin to lightly brown. Mix occasionally.

5. Add the diced oregano and mint and fry for 1 minute. Then add the paprika, turmeric, garlic, salt and pepper. Stir well until the sauce bubbles for a minute and add the tomato paste. Mix in ½ cup of water and cook for 2 minutes on a low heat. Set aside. Reserve a few tablespoons of this sauce for garnish.

**Soup**

6. Drain the soaked beans and add to a large soup pot. Add enough water to cover the beans by 2.5 cm (1″) and bring to the boil. Reduce heat and simmer for 1 hour. Ensure the beans are fully submerged and add more water when necessary. Keep lid of pot slightly ajar to prevent the water boiling over. After the hour, drain beans and add back to the pot.

7. To the cooked beans, add the brown lentils, 4 cups of water and ½ tsp salt. Bring to the boil again. Reduce heat and simmer for 30 minutes, adding extra water as required. The beans should always be covered in the water.

8. Add the bowl of chopped herbs to the cooking beans and another 4 cups of water or enough to just cover the herbs. Let simmer for 20 minutes.

9. Mix in the red sauce and the tagliatelle noodles. Cook for 10 minutes until the noodles are 'al dente'.

10. Mix the flour in a small bowl with ½ cup of water to form a watery paste. Mix into to the soup. Simmer for another 5 minutes. The consistency of the soup should be thick, but if it is too thick, add some extra water. Add extra salt to taste.

Pour hot soup into bowls and add a dollop of yoghurt and some of the reserved red sauce.

*This is a variation of the previous herb and bean noodle soup.*

# herb and wheat soup
## ❧aush-eh perdah❧

 20 mins prep
 1 hr cooking
 Serves 4
 1 srv ≈ 226Cal/945kJ

**SOUP**
½ cup of bulgur wheat (cracked wheat)
3 cups garlic chives diced (or use spring onions)
1 cup silverbeet/chard (diced)
½ cup parsley (diced)
½ cup dill (diced)
1 tsp salt
2 Tbsp flour mixed in ½ cup of water

**RED SAUCE BASE**
1 medium onion (diced)
2 garlic cloves (diced)
½ cup fresh mint (diced)
2 Tbsp tomato paste
1 tsp pepper
1 tsp turmeric
1 Tbsp paprika
¼ cup oil
½ tsp salt

### Red sauce base
1. In a fry pan add ¼ cup of oil and the diced onion. Sauté for 7-8 minutes on medium heat to lightly brown the onions.
2. Add the garlic and diced mint and fry for a minute.
3. Add the paprika, turmeric, salt and pepper. Stir well and let the spices fry for another minute before mixing in the tomato paste. Mix in ½ cup of water and cook for 3 minute without stirring on a low heat.
4. Turn off heat and set aside for later. Reserve a few tablespoons for garnish.

### Soup
5. In a large pot add bulgur wheat, 6 cups of water, 1 tsp of salt and bring to the boil. Do not cover pot with a lid. Let boil on medium heat for 20 minutes. Mix occasionally to prevent wheat from sticking to bottom of the pot.
6. Next add all the chopped chives, silverbeet, parsley and dill and mix through.
7. Let simmer for 20 minutes on low-medium heat, stirring occasionally.
8. In a small cup mix the 2 Tbsp flour with ½ cup of water. Add the flour mixture to the soup. Stir through for a minute to thicken.
9. Finally add the red onion sauce to the soup and simmer for 5 minutes stirring occasionally to prevent the soup sticking to the bottom of the pot. Add extra salt to taste.

Serve soup with a dollop of yoghurt and drizzle with the reserved red sauce.

# pork consommé
## ⌘reesh-ackleh⌘

⧗ 20 mins prep
♨ 4 hrs cooking
🍲 Serves 4
⚛ 1 srv ≈ 320Cal/1339kJ

*The Assyrian name for this recipe literally translates to 'head and feet' and is basically what the recipe calls for. It is a rich stock made from boiling stock friendly bones.*

*The garlic really brings out the flavour of this soup and cuts through the concentrated stock.*

*Lamb shanks and bones can be used instead of pork.*

*This dish is lip smacking goodness.*

### SOUP
500g(1 lb) pork trotters, hock or stock friendly bones.
200g (7oz) beef or pork tripe (optional)
300g (10oz) pork belly slices and/or pork ossobuco
3 bay leaves
3 cloves garlic
1 tsp salt

### GARNISH
2 tsp extra fresh crushed garlic
Bunch of coriander roughly chopped
Bunch of spring onions roughly chopped

1. In a large stock pot add all the pork pieces and tripe and enough water to cover and bring to the boil. Boil for 1 minute then drain.
2. Re-fill with 8 cups of water and bring back to the boil. Turn the heat down to a simmer. Add the salt, whole peeled garlic cloves and bay leaves.
3. Simmer on low heat for 3-4 hours making sure that the water always covers the pork. Add extra water as needed. Note: If you have a pressure cooker, you can cook this on a low heat for 1 hour (making sure you do not add water over the level indicated by the pressure cooker instructions).
4. Take off the heat and let cool. Taste for salt, you may need to add some extra.
5. When cool, sieve the stock into another pot.
6. With the pork solids, discard the fatty bits and bones. Separate out the meat and slice into bite sized pieces. Slice the tripe into neat strips and put this along with the meat back into the strained broth. Skim off any fat.
7. Optionally you can refrigerate the soup. This will let the fat solidify and be easily removed. When refrigerated, the soup will set like jelly.
8. Heat the soup before serving.

In each bowl add ¼ tsp of freshly crushed garlic and pour the hot soup over it. Sprinkle with chopped spring onions and coriander. Dip bread into the broth and enjoy.

*This is a traditional Assyrian dish.*

*This recipe calls for two grades of bulgur wheat: a fine and coarse grade. If you can't find the fine variety don't worry, just use the regular bulgur for the meatball mix.*

# meatball stew
## ᔆchiptehᔆ

 30 mins prep

 1 hr 10 mins cooking

Serves 6

1 srv ≈ 550 Cal / 2300 kJ

**SOUP BASE**
1 cup regular bulgur wheat
1 tsp salt
1 large tomato
1 small green capsicum
3 Tbsp butter

**RED SAUCE**
¼ cup oil
1 medium onion
2 Tbsp tomato paste
2 Tbsp paprika
1 tsp pepper
½ tsp salt

**MEATBALL**
600g (1.3 lb) beef or lamb mince
½ cup fine bulgur wheat
2 Tbsp dried oregano
1 Tbsp dried basil
1 Tbsp dried tarragon
½ cup of diced spring onions
6 small eggs (hard boiled)
1 large egg (raw)
½ tsp salt
Optional: small hot green pepper

## Soup base

1. Add the 1 cup of regular bulgur wheat into a large pot containing 6 cups of water.
2. Add 1 tsp salt, 3 Tbsp butter, the capsicum (whole) and the tomato roughly chopped. Bring to the boil then simmer on low heat for 30 minutes. Mix occasionally. Do not cover pot as it may boil over.

## Making the meatballs

3. Soak ½ cup of the fine bulgur wheat in cold water for 15 minutes.
4. In a large bowl add the minced meat, salt, dried herbs, spring onions, the raw egg and the pre-soaked bulgur wheat above (well drained). If using the hot green pepper, de-seed and finely dice and add to the bowl. Knead this mixture by hand until all the components are well combined.
5. Divide the mince into six equal portions. For each portion, form into a flat disc and place a peeled hard boiled egg in the centre. Mold the meat around the egg to fully cover it. Pinch the ends so that it wont open when cooked. Form into ball shape.
6. Add the meat balls into the pot containing the bubbling wheat soup and simmer for 30 minutes. Add extra water if needed but ensure that the soup is not too thin.

## Red sauce

7. In a separate pan heat the oil. Add the chopped onion and sauté for about 5 minutes. Add tomato paste, paprika, salt and pepper. Cook for 2 minutes.
8. Mix in ½ cup of water and cook for an additional 2 minutes.
9. Add this entire sauce into the meat ball soup, mixing it through.
10. Simmer the soup for another 5 to 10 mins.

For each person, pour a bowl of the soup and add a meatball. Sprinkle with some fresh chopped parsley. Eat with crusty bread.

# rice and lentil chicken soup

**SOUP BASE**
½ cup short grain rice
½ cup brown or green lentils
1 cup flat leaf parsley (chopped)
4 cups of chicken broth
1 lemon

**RED SAUCE**
1 onion (diced finely)
3 Tbsp vegetable oil
2 tsp paprika
2 Tbsp tomato paste
1 tsp salt
½ tsp ground pepper

20 mins prep
50 mins cooking
Serves 4
 1 srv ≈ 252 Cal / 1054 kJ

*For this recipe you could boil a small chicken for an hour to create the broth and then also add the meat to the soup.*

## Soup

**1.** In a large pot add the chicken broth, 4 cups of water, salt and bring to the boil.

**2.** Add the rice and lentils and mix through.

**3.** Turn down the heat and let simmer for 40 minutes. The rice and lentils should always be covered by water. Add extra water if needed.

## Red onion sauce

**4.** While the rice and lentils are simmering, in a separate pan add the oil and the onions. Sauté for about 7 - 8 minutes until the onions begin to lightly brown.

**5.** Add the paprika, pepper and the tomato paste and gently fry for a few more minutes.

**6.** Add ½ cup of water and let simmer for 2 minutes.

## Finishing the soup

**7.** After the lentils and rice has simmered for 40 minutes add the red onion sauce to the pot and stir through.

**8.** Finally add the fresh chopped parsley. Cook for a further 5 mins on low heat.

**9.** Squeeze the juice of one lemon into the pot and stir through. Add extra salt to taste.

Serve hot with plenty of fresh bread.

# Rice

Glorious rice  Fluffy basmati  Delicious dolma

# fluffy basmati rice
## ❧pilau❧

**3 cups basmati rice**
**3 Tbsp vegetable oil**
**3 Tbsp butter**
**2 Tbsp salt**
**Juice of half a lemon**

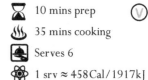

⏳ 10 mins prep    Ⓥ
♨ 35 mins cooking
🍲 Serves 6
⚛ 1 srv ≈ 458 Cal / 1917 kJ

*Rice is a main side dish to many Assyrian meals.*

*It is common to line the base of the cooking pot with slices of potato before the final cooking stage of the rice (step 4). Use 4 Tbsp of oil in the base of the pot before lining with potatoes. This will produce a crispy base. Use a non-stick pot to prevent sticking.*

1. Place the rice in a bowl and add cold tap water. Mix with your hand and drain. Repeat this 3 times.
2. In a large pot fill halfway with water and bring to the boil. Mix in the lemon juice and 2 Tbsp salt. Add the drained, washed rice to the pot, stirring until the water begins boiling again. Let boil for 4 or 5 minutes.
3. Strain the rice in a sieve or colander and rinse under cold tap water.
4. To the empty pot the rice was boiled in, add some oil to cover the base (about 3 Tbsp) and add the drained rice to form a mound. Poke some holes in the rice and sprinkle with ½ cup of water.
5. Put on a tight fitting lid that has been wrapped in a tea towel (see page 161) and cook on a low heat for 20 minutes.
6. Turn the heat off. Top the rice with 3 Tbsp of butter and replace the lid to keep the heat in and let the butter melt through.

Serve this rice alongside any of the dishes in the "Mains" section of this book.

# rice with barberries
## ❧zereshk pilau❧

**¼ tsp saffron**
**¼ cup Zereshk (or use dried cranberries)**
**¼ cup dried black currants**
**¼ cup pine nuts or blanched chopped almonds**
**3 Tbsp butter**

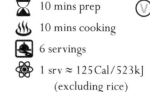

⏳ 10 mins prep    Ⓥ
♨ 10 mins cooking
🍲 6 servings
⚛ 1 srv ≈ 125 Cal / 523 kJ
      (excluding rice)

*Zereshk (barberry) is a small dried berry with a sour taste. You can find these in middle eastern groceries or specialty food stores.*

*If you can't find zereshk, substitute with dried cranberries.*

1. Make rice as per the recipe above. Leave on a very low setting to keep warm.
2. In a small cup add ¼ cup of boiling water and sprinkle the saffron strands over it. Cover the cup with a saucer and let the saffron seep for at least 30 minutes.
3. Melt the butter in a pan and add the zereshk and nuts and stir on low heat to lightly brown the nuts. Add the currants and stir for 5 mins. Take off the heat. Add half of the saffron seeped water and mix through.
4. Take about ¼ cup of the cooked fluffy basmati rice you prepared earlier and put into a small bowl. Add the rest of the saffron seeped water to this rice to colour it. Mix it so that all the rice is bright yellow.

To serve, plate the hot fluffy basmati rice out onto a long serving platter. Sprinkle the yellow saffron rice over the top and then spoon over the zereshk mixture.

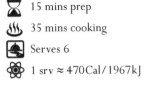
*This red rice with lamb is delicious.*

*You can use beef for this dish if you prefer.*

*Use a low heat when cooking this dish over a stove as it can easily burn. Alternatively it can be baked in the oven.*

# red rice
## ❧riza smooka☙

2 cups basmati rice
500g (1 lb) lamb (cubed leg meat)
1 cup tomato passata (strained tomato)
1 onion (diced)
3 Tbsp vegetable oil
1 Tbsp paprika
1 Tbsp tomato paste
1 tsp salt
½ tsp black pepper

## Prepare the meat

1. Heat oil in a pot and fry the diced onion until translucent.
2. Add the meat. Cook until the meat pieces have browned on all sides (about 5 minutes). Place the lid on the pot and cook on low heat for 20 minutes. Stir occasionally and add some water if it begins to dry out.
3. To the meat, add the salt, pepper, paprika and tomato paste and stir. After a few minutes, add the passata and mix through.
4. Add ½ cup of water. Let simmer gently for a further 5 mins.

## Prepare the rice

5. Bring a separate pot of water to the boil and add the basmati rice. Mix the rice to prevent it clumping together until it begins to boil. Boil for 5 minutes.
6. Drain the rice in a sieve or colander over a sink.
7. Add the strained rice to the pot containing the tomato meat mixture and carefully stir through.
8. Choose one of the following cooking methods:

## Cooking method 1 : Stove top cooking

9. This is a stove top method of cooking the rice. To the pot add a tight fitting lid that has been wrapped in a tea towel (see page 161) and cook on a very low setting for 20 –30 minutes.
10. Check every 10 minutes. If the rice looks very dry, sprinkle over ¼ cup of extra water.
11. When the rice is cooked, turn off the heat.

## Cooking method 2 : Oven baking

12. This is the oven baking method for cooking this dish. After the boiled rice was added to the red meat mixture and mixed through, pour this into an oven proof dish that has a lid. Cook for 30 minutes at 200 °C/400 °F in a reheated oven.

Serve with a simple garden salad (see page 45), gherkins, pickled green peppers and thin slices of red onion.

# rice and chicken
## ৯riza chetetah৩

 20 mins prep

 1 hr cooking

 Serves 6

 1 srv ≈ 920 Cal / 3851 kJ

1 medium sized chicken cut into pieces
2 ½ cups basmati rice
4 Tbsp vegetable oil
1 medium potato (sliced)
2 Tbsp butter
1 tsp salt (+2 Tbsp for boiling rice)
Optional: ¼ tsp saffron

*This simple chicken and rice combination is a family favourite.*

*Tastes great with a dash of hot chilli or Tabasco sauce.*

*The chicken can be either boiled or roasted quickly in the oven before adding it to the rice to cook further.*

### Prepare the chicken

**1.** Cut the chicken into serving sized pieces.

**2.** Cook the chicken using only one of the following methods (boil or bake):
**Method 1:** In a large pot add 3 cups of water and 1 tsp salt. Add the chicken pieces and bring to the boil. Reduce heat to medium/low and cook for 30 minutes. Turn off heat.
**Method 2:** Rub the raw chicken pieces with oil and sprinkle with salt. Place on a foil lined oven tray and cook in a hot oven (230°C/450°F) for 30 minutes. Remove from the oven and let rest.

### Prepare the rice

**3.** Place the rice in a bowl and add cold tap water. Mix with your hand and drain. Repeat this 3 times to remove the excess starch.

**4.** In a large pot (preferably non-stick), fill halfway with water and add 2 Tbsp salt. Bring to the boil. Add the drained rice to the pot. Stir until the water begins boiling again. Boil for 5 mins then strain the rice in a sieve or colander over a sink. Rinse with cold tap water.

### Assemble the dish

**5.** Using the same pot that the rice was boiled in, heat 4 Tbsp of oil on medium heat. Layer the potato slices over the base of the pot and fry for a few minutes. Do not brown.

**6.** Cover the potato slices with half of the cooked and strained rice. Layer the cooked chicken over the rice and cover with the remaining rice.

**7.** Ladle ½ cup of the chicken broth over the rice. If you roasted the chicken, pour ¼ cup of water to any juices left in the oven tray that the chicken was cooked in to deglaze the pan. Pour this liquid over the rice.

**8.** Tie a clean tea towel around the lid of the pot and cover pot firmly (see page 161).

**9.** Reduce the stove heat to low and cook for 20 mins.

**10.** Check rice is cooked by tasting a few grains. Turn off the heat.

**11.** Add 2 Tbsp of butter on top of the rice and replace the lid. The butter will melt though.

To serve, place the rice and chicken onto a platter. Decorate with the crispy potatoes that lined the bottom of the pot. Serve with a fresh garden salad (page 45).

Optional: Soak ¼ tsp of saffron in ¼ cup of boiled water. Leave to seep for at least 15 minutes. Just before serving, sprinkle a little over the rice and partly mix in.

# rice and lamb shank
## ❧riza mahicheh❧

2 lamb shanks (each cut in half)
2 cups basmati rice
4 Tbsp vegetable oil
2 Tbsp butter
1 tsp salt (+2 Tbsp for boiling the rice)

 15 mins prep

 1 hr 30 mins cooking

Serves 4

 1 srv ≈ 717 Cal / 3000 kJ

*It is really important to ensure the lamb is cooked well so that it is soft and falling off the bone.*

*As with other rice dishes, you can line the base of the pot after you have added the oil with strips of pita bread or slices of potato before layering the rice and meat. This produces a nice golden crispy addition to the dish.*

## Prepare the lamb shanks

1. Cook the lamb shanks using only one of the following methods:
   **Method 1:** Add the lamb shanks to a large pot with 3 cups of water and 1 tsp of salt. Bring to the boil. Boil on low heat for 1½ hours. Ensure there is enough water in the pot while it is cooking.
   **Method 2:** Place the lamb shanks in a pressure cooker with about 3 cups of water and 1 tsp salt. Cook on low for 30-40 mins. Turn off and leave to cool.

## Prepare the rice

2. Place the rice in a bowl and add cold tap water. Mix with your hand and drain. Repeat this 3 times to remove the excess starch.

3. In a large pot (preferably non-stick), fill halfway with water and add 2 Tbsp salt. Bring to the boil.

4. Add the drained rice to the pot. Stir until the water begins boiling again. Boil for 5 mins then strain the rice in a sieve or colander over a sink. Rinse with cold tap water.

## Assemble the dish

5. Using the same pot that the rice was boiled in, heat 4 Tbsp of oil on medium heat. Cover the bottom of the pot with half of the cooked rice. Take the cooked lamb shanks and tear apart chunks of the meat and assemble (along with the bones) on top of the rice. Cover with the remaining rice.

6. Ladle ½ cup of broth (left over from cooking of the lamb shank) over the rice.

7. Tie a clean tea towel around the lid of the pot and cover pot firmly (see page 161). On a low heat, simmer the rice for 20 minutes.

8. Check that the rice is cooked and turn off the heat. Add 2 Tbsp of butter on top of the rice, replace the lid to let it melt through.

Serve with a fresh garden salad (page 45) and pickles.

# chicken and broad bean rice
## ⮞chetetah bock-le pilau⮜

1 medium sized chicken
2 ½ cups basmati rice
1 cup fresh dill (finely chopped)
1 cup peeled broad beans (or green garden peas)
1 potato cut in ½ cm slices (¼″ slices)
4 Tbsp vegetable oil
1 tsp salt (+2 Tbsp for boiling the rice)

⧖ 20 mins prep
♨ 1 hr cooking
🍲 Serves 6
⚛ 1 srv ≈ 960 Cal/4019kJ

*Rice and chicken but this time with fresh dill and broad beans.*

*Instead of potatoes at the bottom of the pot you can use strips of pita bread. It will come out golden and crispy.*

*Be adventurous with the presentation. You could place a large platter directly over the pot and flip over. The rice and chicken should pop out in one large piece with crispy potatoes on the top (like an upside down cake). You need to use a non-stick pot otherwise it can get messy!*

## Prepare the chicken

**1.** Cut the chicken into serving sized pieces.

**2.** Cook the chicken using only one of the following methods (boil or bake):

**Method 1:** In a large pot add 3 cups of water and 1 tsp salt. Add the chicken pieces and bring to the boil on medium heat. Cook for 30 minutes. Turn off heat.

**Method 2:** Rub the raw chicken pieces with oil and sprinkle with salt. Place on a foil lined oven tray and cook in a hot oven (230°C/450°F) for 30 minutes. Remove from the oven and let rest.

## Prepare the rice

**3.** Finely chop the dill. For the broad beans, ensure that the beans have been peeled to remove the thick husk that surrounds each individual bean.

**4.** Place the rice in a bowl and add cold tap water. Mix with your hand and drain. Repeat this 3 times to remove the excess starch.

**5.** In a large pot (preferably non-stick), fill halfway with water and add 2 Tbsp salt. Bring to the boil.

**6.** Add the drained rice to the pot. Stir until the water begins boiling again. Boil for 5 mins then strain the rice in a sieve or colander over a sink. Rinse with cold tap water.

**7.** While rice is in the colander, gently fold in the broad beans and finely chopped dill.

## Assembling the dish

**8.** Using the same pot that the rice was boiled in, heat 4 Tbsp of oil on medium heat. Layer the potato slices over the base of the pot and fry for a few minutes. Do not brown.

**9.** Cover the potatoes with half of the green rice. Add a layer of the cooked chicken and cover with the remaining green rice.

**10.** Ladle ½ cup of the chicken broth over the rice. If you roasted the chicken, pour ¼ cup of water to any juices left in the oven tray that the chicken was cooked in to deglaze the pan. Pour this liquid over the rice.

**11.** Tie a clean tea towel around the lid of the pot and cover pot firmly (see page 161).

**12.** Reduce the stove heat to low and cook for 20 mins.

**13.** Before serving, add 2 Tbsp of butter on top of the rice and let it melt through.

Serve with a fresh garden salad (see page 45).

# broad bean and dill rice
## ❧bock-le pilau❧

2 cups basmati rice
1 cup dill (finely chopped)
1 cup broad beans (shelled and peeled)
3 Tbsp vegetable oil
2 Tbsp salt for boiling the rice

⏳ 15 mins prep    Ⓥ
♨ 35 mins cooking
🍲 Serves 4
⚛ 1 srv ≈ 576Cal/2411kJ

*Garden peas or frozen soya beans (edamame) work well with this recipe in place of broad beans.*

1. Place the rice in a bowl and add cold tap water. Mix with your hand and drain. Repeat this 3 times to remove the excess starch.
2. In a large pot (preferably non-stick), fill halfway with water and add 2 Tbsp salt. Bring to the boil. Add the drained rice to the pot. Stir until the water begins boiling again. Boil for 5 mins then strain the rice in a sieve or colander over a sink. Rinse with cold water.
3. Gently fold through the rice the broad beans and finely chopped dill.
4. Using the same pot that the rice was boiled in, heat 3 Tbsp of oil on medium heat. Add the green rice in a mound. Sprinkle ½ cup of water over the rice. Tie a clean tea towel around the lid of the pot and cover pot firmly (see page 161).
5. Reduce the stove heat to low and cook for 20 mins.
6. Before serving, add 2 Tbsp of butter on top of the rice and let it melt through.

This is a great dish served simply with a grilled piece of fish (like salmon) and a fresh garden salad (page 45).

# mixed herb rice
## ❧sabzi pilau❧

2 cups basmati rice
½ cup dill
½ cup garlic chives (or use spring onions)
½ cup coriander
½ cup parsley
3 Tbsp vegetable oil

⏳ 15 mins prep    Ⓥ
♨ 35 mins cooking
🍲 Serves 4
⚛ 1 srv ≈ 460Cal/1925kJ

*This is another variation of a herb infused rice.*

1. Follow the same recipe as above. At step 3, mix in all the finely chopped herbs into the rice and continue with the rest of the steps.

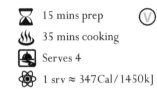

# yoghurt rice
## ❧jurdurr❧

**500g (1 lb) tub of plain natural yoghurt**
**1 cup short grain white rice**
**1 egg**
**1 tsp salt**
**½ Tbsp of butter per person**

⏳ 15 mins prep ⓥ
♨ 35 mins cooking
🍲 Serves 4
⚛ 1 srv ≈ 347 Cal / 1450 kJ

*When you are a bit under the weather and can't keep regular food down, this dish is easy on the stomach and easy to digest.*

*It's also a nutritious breakfast meal and great comfort food when the weather is cold.*

**1.** Add 4 ½ cups of water and 1 tsp salt to a non-stick pot and bring to a boil.

**2.** Stir in the rice and mix until the water begins to boil again. Reduce heat to lowest setting and simmer for 20 minutes.

**3.** Partially cover the pot with the lid to allow steam to escape. Do not fully cover as it will boil over. Mix occasionally to prevent rice from sticking to the bottom of the pot.

**4.** After the 20 minutes, most of the water should have been absorbed into the rice and the rice should be soft and cooked and resemble risotto.

**5.** Beat the yoghurt and egg together and add this directly to the hot, cooked rice. It is important to keep stirring until the rice yoghurt mixture has thickened. It should have the consistency of a porridge.

**6.** Continue stirring for another 5 minutes on a low heat. Add salt to taste. If it is too thick, add a little extra water.

Serve hot. Pour the yoghurt rice into bowls and add a dollop of butter over the top.

# stuffed cabbage and onion
## ❧dolma chalama❧

⧖ 30 mins prep

♨ 2 hrs cooking

🍽 Serves 4

⚛ 1 srv ≈ 418Cal/1750kJ

**WRAPPERS**
½ savoy cabbage
1 large white onion

**FILLING**
1 lamb shank (or 350g/12oz
    lamb or beef cubes)
1 cup short grain rice
1 cup celery leaves
¾ cup flat parsley
½ cup garlic chives
    (or use spring onions)

1 Tbsp curry powder
1 tsp ground black pepper
1 tsp paprika
¼ cup olive oil
2 tsp salt

**TOPPING**
3 Tbsp lemon juice
1 Tbsp sumac (optional)
1 can (400g/14oz) crushed tomatoes

## Preparation
1. Optional: Add 1 Tbsp of sumac to a cup of boiling water. Set aside for later.
2. Boil the lamb shank for 1 hour in 3 cups of water and 1 tsp salt. If using cubed beef or lamb, cook for 30 mins in 1 cup of water. Leave to cool.
3. Remove meat from shank. Roughly dice the meat. Set aside.
4. Cut the core out of the cabbage and separate the cabbage leaves. Try to keep the leaves intact.
5. Add cabbage leaves to a large pot of boiling water along with the whole peeled onion and cook until the leaves are limp (approx. 10 minutes). Leave to cool in the water.

## Prepare filling
6. In a bowl mix together the diced meat, raw rice, diced celery leaves, parsley and spring onions, 1 tsp salt, curry powder, pepper, paprika and olive oil. Stir thoroughly.

## Assemble the dolma
7. To make the cabbage rolls, take a cabbage leaf and slice in half along the large stalk. Fill each leaf with about 2 Tbsp of the rice and herb mixture. Roll the cabbage leaves into small parcels.
8. To make the onion dolmas, peel each layer of the onion in one piece, add 1 Tbsp of rice filling to the center and roll.

## Cooking
9. Add 2 Tbsp oil to a heavy based pot. Line the base of the pot with any torn cabbage leaves. Assemble each cabbage roll neatly in the bottom of the pot to create a layer. Make a layer of onion dolma and continue layering until all the filling has been used.
10. Place the shank bone on the top, it will add flavour.
11. Pour the crushed tomatoes over the dolma in the pot and sprinkle with the lemon juice. Using a strainer, pour the seeped sumac water over the dolma. Discard the sumac leaves. If you are not using sumac, then just add 1 cup of plain water.
12. Place a small flat plate (inverted) onto the dolma (to hold it all in place). Cook gently on a low heat with the lid on the pot for 45 mins to 1 hour.
13. Check after 30 minutes and add extra water if it becomes too dry (½ cup at a time).
14. Test one of the dolma to make sure the rice is fully cooked.

Serve hot. This can be eaten with fresh bread or simply on its own.

*A cabbage roll.*

*An onion roll.*

*This dolma comprises of stuffed summer seasonal vegetables.*

*When choosing your vegetables make sure they are firm and large enough to stuff.*

*Note: This can easily be made a vegetarian dish by simply omitting the lamb.*

*Granny smith apples can also be used in this recipe.*

# summer dolma
## ❧dolma ghedta❧

⏳ 30 mins prep

♨ 2 hrs cooking

🍲 Serves 4

⚛ 1 srv ≈ 418 Cal / 1750 kJ

**VEGETABLES**

4 medium tomatoes

2 medium zucchini (peeled)

2 medium eggplants (peeled)

4 capsicums

**SEASONING**

1 tsp ground black pepper

1 tsp paprika

¼ cup olive oil

2 tsp salt

**FILLING**

1 lamb shank

(or 350g/12oz lamb or beef cubes)

1 cup short grain rice

½ cup fresh parsley

½ cup fresh coriander

½ cup fresh spring onions

½ cup fresh basil

½ cup fresh mint

2 Tbsp fresh tarragon

**Extra oil for frying**

## Make the filling

1. Boil the lamb shank for 1 hour in 3 cups of water and 1 tsp salt. If using cubed beef or lamb, cook for 30 mins in 1 cup of water. Leave to cool.
2. Remove meat from shank. Roughly dice the meat. Set aside.
3. Rinse raw rice in cold water and add to a large bowl along with the chopped lamb, all the herbs (finely chopped), paprika powder, 1 tsp salt, pepper and oil and mix well.

## Hollow out the vegetables

4. Slice the top of the tomatoes (these will be the lids). Scrape out the inside of the tomato removing all the seeds but still leaving the thick wall. Using a pointy knife jab the tomatoes about 2 or 3 times. The tomato scrapping can be added to the filling mixture.
5. Follow the same procedure to hollow out the capsicum, eggplant and zucchini. The zucchini scrapping can also be chopped and added to the filling mixture.
6. Add a few tablespoons of oil to a large pan. Quickly fry outside of zucchini and eggplant until they turn slightly brown. Immediately remove from heat and place on a dish lined with kitchen paper to drain.

## Assembling the dolma

7. Stuff each of the vegetables with the rice and herb mixture. Ensure each vegetable has its own "lid" fitted to contain the rice.

## Cooking

8. Into a large non stick pot add 2 or 3 Tbsp of oil. Layer the stuffed vegetables in the pot.
9. Add 1 cup of water (or broth remaining from the lamb shanks). Place the lamb shank bone over the top, it will add extra flavour to the dish. Put on a tight fitting lid.
10. Cook on a medium heat until the water in the pot begins to bubble then turn the heat down to low. Cook for 1 hour.
11. Cooking is complete when the rice is fully cooked and soft. Add more water if required and keep an eye that it doesn't burn.

Serve with fresh bread or on its own.

*Vegetables hollowed out.*

*Vegetables filled.*

This dolma is the traditional stuffed vine leaves variety.

Fresh picked young vine leaves can be used in place of the preserved variety. When using fresh, you will need about 30-40 leaves. Make sure you wash and inspect each leaf.

Again, as with the other dolma recipes, you can make this vegetarian by just omitting the lamb.

You can also substitute beef instead of lamb if you prefer.

# stuffed vine leaves
## ~dolma darpe~

⏳ 30 mins prep

♨ 1 hr cooking

🍲 Serves 6

⚛ 1 srv ≈ 433Cal/1813kJ

### WRAPPER
500g (1 lb) vine leaves in brine

### FILLING
400g (14oz) leg lamb cubed
1 cup of short grain rice
2 cup coriander (diced)
1 cup dill (diced)
1 cup parsley (diced)
1 cup garlic chives (diced)
    (or use spring onions)
1 cup mint (diced)
3 cloves of garlic (diced)

1 tsp ground black pepper
1 tsp paprika
¼ cup olive oil
2 Tbsp vegetable oil
2 tsp salt

### DRESSING
1 portion of Garlic Yoghurt sauce
1 portion Red Onion sauce
(see page 14)

## Preparation
1. Rinse the vine leaves in cold water to remove excess brine.
2. Finely chop all the herbs and garlic.
3. Rinse the rice under cold water.
4. Heat 2 Tbsp of oil in a small pot and brown the lamb cubes quickly for 5 minutes. Add 1 tsp of salt. Cover pot and reduce heat. Cook slowly for about 20 minutes. The meat will release juices, keep an eye on it so that it doesn't go dry and burn.
5. Once cooked leave to cool, then dice into smaller pea sized pieces.

## Make the filling
6. In a large bowl, mix together the raw rice, diced lamb, diced herbs, garlic, 1 tsp salt, paprika, pepper and olive oil. Mix thoroughly.

## Assemble the Dolma
7. Take a vine leaf with the stem facing upwards (remove stem), and add a spoonful of the meat and herb mixture in the centre. Wrap the vine leaves from top down, then fold over the sides, and continue rolling into small log.
8. In a non-stick pot add 2 Tbsp of oil. Place any torn vine leaves over the base of the pot, then start layering the stuffed vine leaves into the pot.
9. Continue making the dolma until all the rice filling is used.
10. Add 1½ cups of water to the pot. Place a small plate (inverted) on top of the dolma and press it down. Cover pot with lid and cook on a low heat for 45 mins.
11. It is best to check a stuffed vine leaf after 30 minutes of cooking. Add extra water if necessary but not too much. The water should be absorbed by the rice into the dolma. If the rice is cooked then the vine leaves are ready.

Serve the dolma with a dollop of garlic yoghurt and red onion sauce. Eat with fresh bread.

# Mains

Hearty meals eaten with a side of fluffy rice

The cut of meat
must be very
tender. Lamb eye
fillet or loin fillet
are perfect.

If you prefer beef,
use a tender steak
like beef fillet.

Chicken livers can
also be cooked over
the BBQ and are
delicious. Don't
overcook as they
will become dry.
These are best
eaten as soon as
they are cooked.

BBQ lamb is
traditionally
served with rice
and is known as
Chelo Kebab.

# lamb kebabs
## ~du-yah-teh ~

 30 mins prep /
overnight in fridge

 10 mins cooking

 Makes 6 skewers

1 skewer≈235 Cal/982 kJ

**500g (1 lb) lamb eye fillet or loin fillet**
  **(or beef fillet or tender steak cubed)**
**1 large onion**
**¼ cup melted butter for basting**
**Salt**
**Optional: sumac seasoning**

### Prepare meat

1. The night before the barbecue, cut the meat into bite sized cubes. Add to a bowl.
2. Peel and cut the onion in half and then thinly slice Mix into the cubed meat. Onion juice could also be added to marinade the meat (i.e. puree an onion and press into a sieve to squeeze out juice). Cover the bowl with plastic wrap and refrigerate overnight.

### Prepare barbecue

3. Prepare your charcoal barbecue. Remove the metal grill. Use enough charcoal to cover the base of the barbecue. The barbecue is ready when the charcoal is white hot.
4. Skewer the onion marinated meat. Use flat long skewers that are long enough to rest over the barbecue. Brush the skewered meat with some melted butter.
5. Place the lamb kebabs on the barbecue over the direct heat of the coals. You want them to sit about 8 cm (3″) above the charcoal (depending on how hot the barbecue is).
6. Turn skewers over when browned on one side. Cook until the meat has cooked to your liking. It is best not to over cook the meat otherwise it will get dry and tough. It should be a little pink inside. Baste occasionally with melted butter while cooking.
7. Once cooked, take off heat and serve immediately with freshly cooked basmati rice.

To serve, add a dollop of butter on a plate, top with a serving of hot basmati rice (see page 76), arrange a skewer of barbecue lamb and a barbecue tomato (see page 104). Sprinkle with salt and sumac.

Another tradition is to add a raw egg yolk to the plate along with a dollop of butter before topping with the hot rice and meat. Mix the rice before eating with the lamb.

# yoghurt drink
## ~dov-auh~

 2 mins prep (V)

 no cooking

 Serves 1

1 srv ≈ 40 Cal/1671 kJ

**Full cream natural yoghurt**
**Still or sparkling mineral/soda water**
**Dried mint (optional)**
**Salt**

This a refreshing summer drink. Mix 3-4 tablespoons of yoghurt in a glass, add a pinch or two of salt and a pinch of dried mint. Mix well and stir in the ice cold water a bit at a time to fill the glass.

# minced kebabs
## ❧du-yah-teh gireesah❧

500g (1 lb) minced lamb
1 egg
1 medium brown onion
1 tsp bicarbonate of soda
1 tsp salt
Optional: sumac seasoning

⧖ 30 mins prep /
30 mins in fridge

♨ 10 mins cooking

🍳 Makes 6 skewers

⚛ 1 skewer≈236 Cal / 989 kJ

*This is probably the most difficult recipe in this book to get right. You will need flat and wide kebab skewers (known as a shish or seekh).*

*If the lamb is too fatty, there will be a lot of flare ups on the barbecue. Use a minced lamb that is about 10-15% fat (20% max).*

*Note that the BBQ grate needs to be removed. The skewers should rest above the hot coal (about 10 cm/4" above the coals).*

*Before cooking all the skewers at once, practice with one or two skewers to ensure you get the cooking technique right.*

*These can be eaten straight off the barbecue wrapped in some pita bread with garlic sauce, hummus, lettuce and tomato.*

*They are delicious sprinkled with sumac.*

1. Prepare your barbecue. Remove the metal grill and ensure that the skewers are long enough to rest over the barbecue (see photo on left). The barbecue is ready when the charcoal is white hot.

## Kebab mixture

2. Finely grate the onion and squeeze out as much juices as you can. A quick way of grating the onion is to roughly chop and then use a stick blender to blend to a fine puree. Place in a sieve and squeeze out the juice by pressing down with the back of a spoon. Set aside the onion solids for step 4. Keep the juice as it will be used to form the kebabs in step 6. The juice could also be used as a marinade for the lamb kebabs recipe (page 98).

3. Add minced lamb to a large stainless steel bowl or pot and place over a very low heat on the stove. Knead with one hand for a minute until the meat starts to warm up. You do not want to cook the meat. Your hand should never get hot. You want to melt the fat slightly while working the meat. Turn off the heat and continue kneading the meat for 6-8 minutes until the meat consistency is smooth and the colour changes to a pale pink.

4. Add the grated onion solids, egg, bicarbonate of soda and salt. Knead for a further 5 minutes. It will be smooth and sloppy. You want it very well blended.

5. Refrigerate this for at least 30 minutes so that it firms up and the fat resolidifies. This is an important step otherwise the meat will fall off the skewers.

## Forming the kebabs

6. When ready to cook, moisten hand in the reserved onion juice (add extra water if there is not enough liquid to moisten hand) and take a palm full of the meat.

7. Shape around the skewer to form a flat sausage shape. The kebabs should be approximately 20 cm (8") long. Taper the ends to prevent the meat falling off when cooking over the coals. There should be enough meat for 6 skewers.

## Cooking

8. When the charcoal is white hot, place the skewers onto the barbecue ensuring that the full lengths of the kebabs have the direct heat of the charcoal. You want the skewers to sit about 8-10 cm (3-4") above the coals (depending on how hot the coals are).

9. It is important to turn the skewers over as soon as the kebabs turn pale. This can happen within a minute. It is important to seal the meat around the skewer to prevent it from falling off. Once sealed, turn over frequently to cook on each side. Brush with melted butter after kebabs begin to brown.

10. When the kebabs are a nice dark brown colour, they are ready to be removed from the skewers. You can use fresh pita (flat bread) to slide the kebabs off the skewers.

Serve immediately with white basmati rice (see page 76) and barbecued tomatoes and peppers (see page 104). Sprinkle with sumac.

# chicken kebabs
## ❧ju-jeh kebab↩

1 kg (2.2 lb) chicken wings
¼ cup lemon juice
1 Tbsp natural yoghurt
4 cloves of garlic (crushed)
¼ tsp of saffron strands
Salt

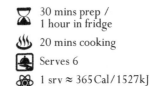

30 mins prep /
1 hour in fridge

20 mins cooking

Serves 6

1 srv ≈ 365 Cal / 1527 kJ

1. Cut the chicken wings at the joints to create smaller pieces.
2. To the raw chicken pieces add the lemon juice, yoghurt, garlic and saffron. Mix well and let marinade for an hour in the fridge.
3. Prepare your barbecue.
4. Skewer the chicken pieces and place over the white-hot coal. Turning regularly to prevent burning. If you find they are cooking too quickly and burning, you will need to raise them further away from the coals to reduce the direct heat.
5. When the chicken is golden and cooked through, remove from skewers, sprinkle with salt and serve.

These kebabs are usually served as part of a barbecue buffet that includes minced lamb kebabs, lamb cubed kebabs, barbecued tomatoes, peppers, rice and plenty of salads.

*Every barbecue needs some juicy garlicky chicken wings.*

*Chicken thighs and small drumsticks work well with this recipe too and of course you could use boneless chicken breast.*

*For large pieces of chicken move them further away from the coal's heat to give them enough time to cook through.*

*Having a
barbecued tomato
along with lamb or
chicken kebabs is a
Persian tradition.*

# vegetable kebabs

**6 large tomatoes**
**6 green Romano peppers**
**3 capsicum (bell peppers)**
**¼ cup olive oil**
**salt**

⌛ 10 mins prep   Ⓥ
♨ 10 mins cooking
🍲 Serves 6
⚛ 1 srv ≈ 143 Cal/600kJ

**1.** Deseed and cut the capsicum into quarters. Slice the Romano peppers in half lengthwise and deseed as well.
**2.** Skewer the tomatoes, Romano peppers and capsicums separately.
**3.** Barbecue them over hot charcoal until soft and cooked through and slightly charred.
**4.** Place the Romano peppers and capsicum into a bowl and drizzle with the olive oil and sprinkle with salt.
**5.** The tomatoes can be placed in a separate bowl and sprinkled with salt.

Barbecued vegetables are traditionally served as a side dish with the lamb and chicken kebabs along with basmati rice (see page 76) .

# meatball casserole
## ❧khoorosht'd koofteh reece❧

⧖ 15 mins prep

♨ 50 mins cooking

🍲 Serves 4

⚛ 1 srv ≈ 454 Cal/1902 kJ

*This meatball stew is served with white basmati rice, however you could serve this on top of spaghetti too.*

*Try adding a little chilli powder for some extra heat.*

**MEATBALL MIX**
500g (1 lb) mince meat (beef or lamb)
1 medium onion (grated)
1 egg (large)
½ tsp salt

**CASSEROLE**
1 large onion (diced)
3 Tbsp vegetable oil
1 Tbsp tomato paste
1 Tbsp paprika (or mild paprika powder)
400g/14oz can of crushed tomato or passata
2 cups water
½ tsp black ground pepper
¼ cup parsley (diced)
½ tsp salt
Juice of 1 lemon

## Meatball mix

1. In a large bowl add the mince meat, the grated onion, egg and ½ tsp salt.
2. Mix together thoroughly by hand. The meat should have a smooth consistency. Set aside in the fridge while preparing the casserole.

## Casserole

3. In a pot, sauté the diced onion in the oil until translucent (about 5 minutes).
4. Add the paprika, black pepper, ½ tsp salt and tomato paste. Fry together gently for a minute.
5. Add 2 cups of water and the crushed tomato, and bring the sauce to the boil. Reduce heat to low.

## Assemble the casserole

6. Take the meatball mix and make small golf-ball sized meatballs and drop directly into the bubbling sauce.
7. Simmer for 20 - 30 mins until the meat balls are fully cooked. You may need to add extra water (½ to 1 cup). The soup of this casserole should have a thick saucy consistency.
8. Once cooked mix through the chopped parsley and squeeze the juice of one lemon directly into the casserole. Add extra salt to taste.

Serve this with plain basmati rice (page 76) and a garden salad (page 45).

# okra casserole
## ✑khoorosht'd bomya✑

⧖ 15 mins prep

♨ 50 mins cooking

⊞ Serves 4

⚛ 1 srv ≈ 462 Cal / 1936 kJ

500g (1 lb) boneless leg of lamb (cubed)
250g (½ lb) of okra (tops trimmed)
3 Tbsp vegetable oil + 3Tbsp extra
1 large onion
2 Tbsp tomato paste
1 tsp black pepper
1 Tbsp paprika
1 tsp salt
Juice of 1 lemon
Handful of coriander for garnish

*The basis to every good Assyrian casserole is the onion, paprika and tomato paste mix.*

*With recipes that call for paprika, a mild or hot paprika can be used depending on your palate.*

*While lamb is traditionally used in these casseroles, you can substitute beef if you prefer.*

1. In a heavy based pot, heat 3 Tbsp vegetable oil.
2. Add the lamb cubes and brown on all sides (3 minutes).
3. Add salt and reduce heat and put the lid on the pot. Cook for a further 10-15 minutes. The meat will begin releasing its juices.
4. Add the diced onions to the meat and cook for a further 5 - 8 mins. Mix occasionally.
5. Add the tomato paste, pepper and paprika and cook for a few minutes. You want to evenly coat the meat pieces while gently frying the spices.
6. Add 2 cup of water and let it simmer for 10 minutes.
7. While the meat is simmering, in a separate fry pan add 3 Tbsp of oil and gently pan fry the Okra. They should just begin to colour (approx. 5-8 minutes).
8. Add the okra directly to the stewing meat and simmer gently for a further 15 –20 minutes.
9. Squeeze the juice of 1 lemon into the pot (depending on taste). Sprinkle with coriander and stir through.

Serve hot on top of plain basmati rice (see page 76).

# green bean casserole
## ✑khoorosht'd laubya✑

Follow above recipe but substitute 4 cups of green string beans in place of the okra (cut on a diagonal into 2.5 cm / 1″ pieces).

# celery casserole
## ✑khoorosht'd charaffs✑

Follow above recipe but substitute 4 cups of chopped celery stalk in place of the okra (cut into 1¼ cm / ½″ pieces).

# chicken curry
## ☙khoorosht'd curree☙

*Curry is
a family favourite.*

*This recipe is
very versatile and
you can replace
the chicken with
fish or prawns.*

*Lamb or beef can
be used too, but
you will need to
cook it for longer
until the meat is
soft and tender.*

500g (1 lb) chicken thigh meat pieces
3 Tbsp vegetable oil
1 large onion (diced)
3 cloves garlic crushed
3 Tbsp curry powder
1 tsp paprika
1 tsp pepper
1 Tbsp tomato paste
1 cup crushed tomatoes (canned or fresh)
1 tsp salt
3 Tbsp coriander chopped for garnish

3 medium potatoes (500g / 1 lb)
Oil for frying the potatoes

1. Sauté the diced onions in 3 Tbsp of oil in a large pot for about 5 minutes.
2. Add the chicken pieces to the onions and stir fry for 5 mins on medium heat.
3. Add paprika, pepper, curry powder, salt and the tomato paste. Fry for 2 mins.
4. Mix in the cup of crushed tomatoes and 1 cup of water and bring to a simmer. Let the curry cook for a further 10 minutes.
5. Peel and cut the potatoes into bite sized cubes. Deep fry until golden brown. Drain the potatoes on kitchen paper and set aside.
6. When you are about to serve, add the fried potatoes to the curry and mix through. Add extra water if the curry becomes too thick.
7. Cook for 2 mins before sprinkling the top of the curry with the diced fresh coriander. Stir through.

Serve curry on top of fresh, fluffy basmati rice (see page 76).

# herb lamb with black-eyed peas
## ❧gormeh subzi❧

⌛ Overnight soaking

♨ 1 hr 40 mins cooking

🍽 Serves 4

⚛ 1 srv ≈ 518 Cal/2168 kJ

500g (1 lb) boneless leg of lamb (cubed)
½ cup black eyed peas
1 large onion (diced)
2 Tbsp vegetable oil +4 Tbsp extra
3 cups parsley (diced)
3 cups garlic chives (diced)
1 cup fresh fenugreek leaves diced (or ½ tsp ground fenugreek seeds)
4 preserved dried lemons
1 Tbsp tomato paste
2 tsp turmeric
2 tsp salt
1 tsp black pepper

1. Firstly soak the black-eyed peas in water overnight.
2. In a pot add the 2 Tbsp vegetable oil and sauté the diced onion until softened (about 5 minutes).
3. Add the cubed lamb and 1 tsp salt and mix through. Reduce the heat and put the lid on the pot. Cook on medium low heat for 15 minutes. The lamb should release a lot of liquid and begin to reduce down.
4. To the lamb add 3 cups of water and the drained black-eyed peas. Bring to a slow boil on medium heat.
5. In a separate pan, heat the 4 Tbsp oil and gently fry all the fresh herbs for 5-8 minutes. The volume of the herbs will reduce by a half.
6. To the pot containing the boiling lamb and peas, add tomato paste, 1 tsp salt, turmeric, pepper (and the ground fenugreek if you are not using the fresh leaves). Add an extra cup of water.
7. Add all the fried fresh herbs to the rest of the ingredients in the pot.
8. Add the preserved lemons whole (to be removed later when serving).
9. Simmer this gently on a low heat for 1 hour to allow the flavors to meld together. Stir occasionally. Ensure the lid of the pot is slightly ajar to allow steam to escape.
10. Just before serving, cut the preserved lemons in half so that they release their acidity to the dish. Mix through and let simmer gently for another 5 minutes. Remove the preserved lemons before serving.

Serve over hot, fluffy plain basmati rice (see page 76).

*This is one of the famous Persian dishes that every Persian household cooks. It is also popular in Assyrian households.*

*You can use beef instead of lamb if you prefer.*

*The ingredient that gives this dish that unique taste is the fresh fenugreek leaves. This ingredient may be difficult to find, but ground fenugreek seeds is a good substitute.*

*My mother's garden is always full of herbs. She grows fenugreek with seeds purchased from the spice section of the supermarket.*

*Like most of the stews in this book, it tastes even better heated up the next day.*

The subtle flavour
of cinnamon with
prunes and carrot
really compliment
each other.

Beef can be used
instead of lamb
if you prefer.

Like all the mains
in this section, this
is served on top
of freshly cooked
plain basmati rice.

# prune casserole
## ✎khoorosht'd ahloo✎

500g (1 lb) boneless leg of lamb (cubed)
3 Tbsp + 2 Tbsp vegetable oil
350g (12oz) dried pitted black prunes
3 medium carrots (500g/17½oz)
1 Tbsp tomato paste
1 large onion (diced)
1 tsp ground black pepper
1 tsp paprika
½ cup chopped parsley
1 tsp salt
1 stick of cinnamon

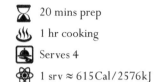

20 mins prep

1 hr cooking

Serves 4

1 srv ≈ 615Cal/2576kJ

1. In a pot, sauté the diced onion in 3 Tbsp oil for 5 minutes until they begin to go translucent. Add the lamb cubes and salt. Brown the meat and place the lid on the pot.
2. Cook on a low heat for 15 minutes. Keep an eye on it so that it doesn't dry out and burn.
3. Add pepper, paprika and tomato paste and stir through, frying gently for a minute.
4. Add 1½ cups of water to the pot and then add the prunes and cinnamon stick. Mix the stew while it comes up to the boil. Turn the heat down to low.
5. Simmer gently for 20 minutes with lid on pot.
6. Cut the carrots into 5 cm (2″) strips.
7. In a separate pan, fry the carrots in 2 Tbsp oil until they have softened slightly but still retain their shape and have gained some colour (about 5 - 8 mins on medium heat).
8. Add the carrots into the pot containing the meat and prunes.
9. Simmer gently for a further 15 mins on low heat. You can add a little extra water if the casserole becomes too thick.
10. Just prior to serving, add the chopped parsley and stir through.

This dish is served over freshly prepared plain basmati rice (see page 76).

# mushroom casserole
## ❧khorusht jubulajeh❧

500g (1 lb) cubed lamb or beef
3 Tbsp vegetable oil
1 medium onion (diced)
500g (1 lb) button mushrooms
1 Tbsp tomato paste
½ tsp black pepper
1 Tbsp mild paprika powder
1 tsp salt

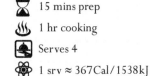

15 mins prep
1 hr cooking
Serves 4
1 srv ≈ 367Cal/1538kJ

*Button mushrooms are used in this recipe, but you can use other varieties. Even canned mushrooms may be used.*

*Portobello, shiitake, king or oyster mushrooms or a combination of these work well with this recipe.*

1. Heat oil in a large pot and add the cubed meat and salt. Quickly brown on all sides and place the lid on the saucepan. Reduce heat and cook for 10-15 mins. The meat should release liquid and begin boiling in its own juices.
2. Add the onions and fry for another 5 minutes until the onions are translucent.
3. Add the pepper, paprika and tomato paste to the meat. Fry the spices for about 2 minutes before stirring through 1 cup of water.
4. Add all the quartered mushrooms and mix through. Turn the heat down to low and simmer gently for 40 minutes with lid of the pot partially ajar to allow steam to escape. Add extra water if needed.

This dish is best served over freshly cooked plain basmati rice (see page 76).

# tomato and eggplant casserole
## ◈khoorosht'd bodemjon◈

500g (1 lb) boneless leg of lamb (cubed)
500g (1 lb) eggplants
500g (1 lb) tomatoes
3 romano peppers (or 2 capsicum)
2 Tbsp vegetable oil + 3 Tbsp extra
2 tsp turmeric
2 tsp black pepper
1 tsp salt

*This dish will become a family favourite.*

*In the Persian language, the word for eggplant and the word for tomato is the same. They are both called bodemjon.*

*So this dish literally translates to "tomato casserole".*

*The long thin type of eggplants work well in this recipe.*

*Beef can be used instead of lamb if you prefer.*

## Prepare the vegetables.

**1.** Peel the eggplants and slice into 1 cm (½″) thick slices length wise or cut into quarters lengthwise depending on their size. Sprinkle liberally with salt and place in a colander over the sink to drain. Leave for at least an 1 hour for the salt to draw out excess moisture.

**2.** Peel the tomatoes by placing them in a bowl of boiling hot water for a minute. Remove from the water and cool before peeling. The skin should peel off easily. Slice the tomatoes into thick pieces.

**3.** Cut the green peppers in half length wise, removing the tops and seeds. Cut into large chunky pieces.

**4.** After the eggplant has been left for an hour to leach out excess water, wipe each piece with a clean tea towel to remove excess salt and water.

**5.** Heat 3 Tbsp of oil in a fry pan and fry the eggplants. Once they are golden brown, remove from pan and place onto a plate. The eggplant will soak up oil so you may need to add extra oil when frying the rest of the eggplants.

## Cook the meat

**6.** Heat 2 Tbsp oil in a large pot and add the cubed lamb. Quickly brown on all sides then place the lid on the saucepan and reduce heat. Cook for 10-15 mins. The meat should release liquid and begin boiling in its own juices.

**7.** Remove the lamb cubes from the pot and set aside.

## Assemble the casserole

**8.** In the same pot the meat was cooked in, place a third of the meat first, then a layer of tomato slices, eggplant and green pepper. Sprinkle with a third of the turmeric, pepper and salt. Repeat layering the next third of the ingredients and spices and then the final layer.

**9.** Add ½ cup of water to the pot. Turn the heat down to low and simmer gently for 30-40 minutes with lid of the pot partially ajar to allow steam to escape. Do not stir.

This casserole is served over fluffy basmati rice (see page 76).

*This lamb ragout dish is best served for supper on cold winter nights.*

*Instead of lamb chops you can use 500g / 1 lb of cubed boneless lamb or beef.*

*Eat with fresh bread.*

# lamb ragout
## ❧tuskebob❧

8 lamb chops
2 Tbsp vegetable oil
1 zucchini
1 eggplant
2 medium tomatoes
1 large carrot
4 large mushrooms
1 long Romano pepper
2 large potatoes
1 small bunch of flat parsley (for garnish)
1 tsp turmeric
1 tsp black pepper
1 tsp salt

30 mins prep

1 hr cooking

Serves 4

1 srv ≈ 733 Cal / 3069 kJ

1. Heat the oil in a pot and quickly brown the chops on each side. Place the chops on a plate and set aside.
2. You can peel the eggplant and zucchini or leave the skin on if you like. Cut all vegetables into 1 cm (½″) thick slices.
3. In a large pot, add a third of the vegetables, sprinkle with some of the turmeric black pepper and salt, and press down with three lamb chops.
4. Repeat with the remaining vegetables, meat and spices.
5. Add ½ cup of water to the pot and begin heating on a medium/low heat for 40 mins with the lid slightly ajar.
6. Before serving add the chopped fresh parsley to the pot and gently stir it through ensuring all the spices and meat are mixed. Cook for a further 5 mins.

Serve by placing the mixed vegetables on each plate and two lamb chops over it. Eat with fresh bread.

120

*Fesenjun is a famous Persian dish made with duck cooked for hours with pomegranate molasses and walnuts. This recipe is a lighter take on that traditional version.*

*You can use this recipe with duck or game birds. Adjust the cooking time to ensure the bird is cooked through.*

# pomegranate and walnut roast chicken

1 large chicken
½ portion of walnut pesto (page 29)
2 Tbsp vegetable oil
1 large onion
2 Tbsp pomegranate molasses or 1 cup of pomegranate juice
Small piece of cinnamon stick (2.5 cm/1″)
½ tsp salt
1 tsp sugar (optional)

30 mins prep
1 hr 10 mins baking
Serves 4
1 srv ≈ 976Cal/4089kJ

## Prepare chicken

1. To prepare the chicken, stuff half of the pesto under the skin (from the head side of the chicken) over the chicken breast. Add the rest of the pesto into the cavity of the chicken.
2. Place in a hot oven (220°C/430°F) for 30 minutes.
3. After the 30 minutes, add the roughly chopped onions into the baking pan with the chicken. Reduce heat (180 °C/360°F) and cook for 40 minutes.
4. Pierce the leg of the chicken and make sure the juice runs clear.
5. Once cooked, remove from the roasting pan and leave to rest for about 10 minutes. Remove the pesto from inside the chicken cavity for the sauce.

## Pomegranate sauce

6. Add 1 cup of water (or pomegranate juice) to the roasting pan which still contains the roasted onions and chicken juices. Scrape all the cooked bits from the pan to collect all the flavours.
7. In another small pot add the pesto that was removed from the chicken cavity and begin to fry for 2 minutes. Carefully pour all the liquid and onions bits from the baking pan into the pot.
8. If using pomegranate molasses, add this to the sauce. Drop in the cinnamon stick and simmer on a low heat for 10-15 minutes to create a reduced sauce.
9. Once the sauce has reduced, discard the cinnamon stick.
10. Use a hand blender to puree the sauce. If it is too thick, add a little extra water. It should have a thick gravy-like consistency. Add salt to taste. If the sauce is a little too sour for your taste, add 1 teaspoon of sugar.

## Assemble dish

11. Cut the chicken into pieces and arrange onto a serving platter. Pour any juices remaining into the pomegranate sauce and mix through. Just before serving, pour the pomegranate sauce over the chicken.

This can be served over plain basmati rice (page 76) and/or with a fresh garden salad (see page 45).

# spaghetti
## ❧mahcaron❧

500g (1 lb) packet of dried spaghetti
500g (1 lb) minced meat (lamb or beef)
200g (7oz) mushrooms (sliced)
1 large onion (diced)
2 Tbsp vegetable oil
2 tsp sweet paprika
½ tsp chilli powder
1 Tbsp tomato paste
1½ cups passata (strained tomato puree)
½ tsp salt
½ tsp pepper

15 mins prep
50 mins cooking
Serves 6
1 srv ≈ 493 Cal / 2064 kJ

*This is our mum's spaghetti recipe and is a family favourite.*

1. In a pot, sauté the diced onion in the oil for 5 minutes until the onions become translucent.

2. Add the mince meat and stir through the onions. Cook the meat for 10 - 15 minutes or until well browned.

3. Add the salt, pepper, chilli powder, paprika, tomato paste. Mix well and cook for a further minute.

4. Mix in the passata and add the sliced mushrooms. Cook for a further 5 mins on medium heat. Add 1 cup of water, stir through and let simmer on low heat for 20 minutes with the lid of the pot slightly ajar.

5. Add the pasta to a large pot of boiling water. Cook until the pasta is 'al dente' (as per instructions on pack).

6. Drain the pasta. Add it to the meat and mushroom mixture and stir through. Let simmer for a further 5 mins on low heat.

Serve with a sprinkle of freshly grated Parmesan cheese and a sprig of basil.

The meat pie is an Australian favourite. It is not hard to be influenced by this traditional meal.

*This is mum's version and we all love it.*

# steak and mushroom pie

500g (1 lb) mince (beef or lamb)
500g (1 lb) portabella mushrooms (sliced)
1 large onion (diced)
2 Tbsp vegetable oil
1 tsp ground black pepper
1 tsp salt
3 Tbsp flour
300g (10oz) puff pastry
    (or bread dough. See page 134)
Glaze: 1 egg + 1 Tbsp natural yoghurt

40 mins prep

1hr stove + 40 min oven

Serves 6

1 srv ≈ 422Cal/1767kJ

## Making the filling

**1.** In a large pot sauté the onions in 2 Tbsp oil until translucent (about 5 minutes). Add the mince meat, stirring well and cook for 15 minutes. Add salt and pepper.

**2.** Add the sliced mushroom and 1 cup of water. Mix through and cook on low heat for 40 minutes. Mix occasionally to prevent sticking to bottom of pot.

**3.** In a separate bowl mix the 3 Tbsp of flour with ½ cup of water to form a loose paste. Add this to the meat mixture. Stir through. Cook for a further 5 minutes to thicken. If it becomes too thick, add a little more water.

**4.** Leave filling to cool to room temperature.

## Assembling the pie

**5.** Preheat oven to 180°C/350°F.

**6.** Grease a large square pie dish and line with a single sheet of the puff pastry. Ensure that pastry covers the side and edges of the dish. Use extra pastry as needed.

**7.** Fill the pastry case with the cooled meat mixture. Place the remaining pastry sheet on top of the meat to completely cover, crimping the edges.

**8.** If you are using the bread dough on page 134, divide in two and roll out to use to line the pie dish and to top the pie. Also let the pie rest for 10 minutes before cooking.

**9.** Crack an egg into a separate bowl and stir in 1 Tbsp of yoghurt. Brush over the pie. Poke a few holes in the top to allow steam to escape.

## Cooking

**10.** Cook in the pre-heated oven for 30-40 mins or until the top of the pie is a golden brown.

Serve with steamed vegetables, mash and plenty of tomato ketchup.

# Pastries & dessert

**Sweet pastries and desserts. Try with a hot chai.**

*This is a traditional Assyrian pastry. It is eaten with sweetened brewed tea.*

*This pastry is unusual in that it is not sweet but has a salty roux filling.*

*My mum insists on using self raising flour even though yeast is used.*

# roux filled pastry
## ⊱cha-deh⊰

⏳ 1 hr 40 mins prep  Ⓥ
♨ 20 mins baking
🍽 12 slices
⚛ 1 srv ≈ 268Cal/1125kJ

**DOUGH**
2 ½ cups self raising flour
½ cup natural yoghurt
60g (2.2oz) melted butter
1 tsp dry yeast
½ cup milk (lukewarm)
1 tsp salt
1 tsp sugar

**FILLING**
½ cup vegetable oil
    (or clarified butter)
1 ¼ cups plain flour
½ tsp salt

**GLAZE**
1 egg yolk
1 tsp yoghurt
1 tsp flour

## Dough

1. In a large bowl mix together the warm milk, yeast, sugar and 1 Tbsp of flour. Set aside in a warm place for 10 minutes to activate the yeast.
2. Into the yeast mixture, mix in the yoghurt and melted butter.
3. Add the flour and salt to form a dough. Knead for 5-8 minutes either by hand or use a stand mixer with dough hook attachments. The dough should be smooth and elastic.
4. Place the dough in a bowl, cover and leave in a warm place for an hour to double in size.

## Filling

5. Heat the oil in a stainless steel pot. Add the flour carefully, mixing continuously. Add the salt.
6. Keep mixing with a wooden spoon while on medium heat for up to 5 minutes. It should begin to go blonde in colour and loosen and have the consistency of peanut butter.
7. Take off the heat and leave to cool completely.

## Shaping the loaves

8. Preheat oven to 200°C/400°F .
9. Knock the air out of the dough and lightly knead. Divide the dough into 2 balls.
10. Take a ball of dough and roll out like a pizza base into a slightly oval shape about 30 cm (12″) long. Take a half of the cooled filling mixture and spread evenly over half the rolled out dough (Fig 1). Fold the other half of the dough over to resemble a half moon. Crimp the edges to lock in the filling (Fig 2).
11. Using a fork, pierce the top evenly (Fig 3). Take a small cup and press down over the top to form a regular pattern (Fig 4).
12. Repeat with the second ball of the dough using the rest of the filling. Place loaves onto a floured oven tray and leave to prove for 20 minutes in a warm place.

## Cooking

13. Create the glaze by mixing the egg yolk, yoghurt and flour, and brush the loaves evenly.
14. Cook for 10-15 minutes in the oven or until golden brown. Take out and leave to cool on a wire rack. Each loaf can be cut into six serving sized pieces (Fig 5).

This pastry is always served with freshly brewed sweet tea. On its own it can be a little dry. You can also spread a little butter on top when eaten for breakfast.

*Fig 1*

*Fig 2*

*Fig 3*

*Fig 4.*

*Fig 5.*

This is another traditional Assyrian pastry which is served alongside freshly brewed tea.

These freeze really well. Once they have cooled from the oven, place them in freezer bags or an airtight container and freeze. To defrost, pop into a warm oven for 10 minutes or microwave for 10-15 seconds.

# sweet layered biscuits
## ❧noz-oo-jeh❧

⏳ 40 mins prep   Ⓥ
♨ 20 mins baking
🍳 Makes: 26 biscuits
⚛ 1 biscuit≈140Cal/586kJ

**DOUGH**
3 cups self raising flour
2 eggs
½ cup caster sugar
¼ cup vegetable oil
½ cup natural yoghurt
½ tsp sodium bicarbonate
1 tsp vanilla essence
2 Tbsp melted butter

**FILLING A**
¼ cup vegetable oil
½ cup caster sugar
½ cup plain flour

**FILLING B**
1 cup shelled walnuts
½ cup caster sugar

**GLAZE**
1 egg yolk
½ Tbsp yoghurt
1 tsp flour

## Filling
**1.** Choose a filling type for this recipe: Filling A or Filling B. For filling A, mix the oil, sugar and flour together. It should have the consistency of peanut butter.
**2.** For filling B, add the sugar and walnuts into a food processor and blend into a crumbly paste-like mixture.

## Dough
**3.** Separate the eggs. Whisk the egg whites to form stiff peaks and set aside.
**4.** In another bowl, using a stand or hand held mixer, beat the egg yolks, vanilla and sugar until they turn a creamy lemony colour (about 5 mins).
**5.** Add the whisked egg whites to the yolk mixture. Beat until fully incorporated.
**6.** Slowly pour in the oil, beating until the oil has completely mixed in.
**7.** Mix together the yoghurt and bicarbonate, and gradually beat into the egg mixture.
**8.** Mix in the self raising flour a little at a time with a wooden spoon. Use just enough to form a very soft dough. Lightly knead for a few minutes. Do not overwork the dough.

## Shaping the biscuits
**9.** Preheat the oven to 180°C/360°F.
**10.** Cut the dough into 2 equal portions.
**11.** Take a portion and roll out onto a lightly floured bench into an oblong shape about 4 mm (¼″) in thickness (see Fig 1).
**12.** Brush with melted butter. Take half of the filling and spread evenly over two thirds of the dough (see Fig 2). Fold the uncovered section of the dough over the filled section (see Fig 3) and then fold over the top (see Fig 4).
**13.** Roll this out again into an oblong shape, this time brush only with melted butter and fold again into thirds as described above. Set aside.
**14.** Repeat steps 11, 12 and 13 with the other dough portion, using the rest of the filling.
**15.** Rollout each of the layered dough to a thickness of about 1 cm (½″). Pierce the dough with a fork to create a pattern over the surface. Use a knife to cut into biscuit sized triangles or squares or you can use a cookie cutter.
**16.** Make the glaze by mixing together the yolk, yoghurt and flour, and brush each biscuit. Place on a baking paper lined cookie tray.

## Cooking
**17.** Bake for 10-15 mins, or until they turn golden brown in colour.
**18.** Cool the biscuits on a wire rack.

Serve with freshly brewed tea or coffee.

*Fig 1.*

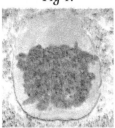
*Fig 2.*

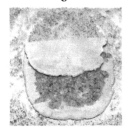
*Fig 3.*

*Fig 4.*

This standard bread recipe can be used to make flat loaves, pizza bases, pie crusts, focaccia or just regular round bread buns.

*It is a very versatile dough.*

# plain bread
## ⌘lakhma⌘

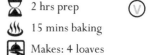

⏳ 2 hrs prep  Ⓥ

♨ 15 mins baking

🍞 Makes: 4 loaves

⚛ 1 loaf ≈ 380 Cal / 1590 kJ

DOUGH

2½ cups plain flour

1 tsp dried yeast

1 cup water (lukewarm)

1 Tbsp yoghurt

1 tsp sugar

2 Tbsp melted butter

½ tsp salt

GLAZE

1 egg beaten with 1 tsp yoghurt

Sesame seeds for garnish

1. In a large bowl mix together the warm water, yeast, sugar and 2 Tbsp of flour. Set aside in a warm place for 10 minutes to activate the yeast. It will begin to froth.
2. To the yeast mixture, mix in the yoghurt and melted butter.
3. Sift the flour and salt together and add this to the liquid to form a dough. Knead this dough for 5 - 10 minutes until smooth and elastic. You can use a stand mixer with dough hooks to knead the dough.
4. Cover the dough with cling film and set in a warm place for an hour. The dough will double in size.
5. After the dough has risen, knock out the air and knead for a few minutes.
6. Divide into 4 balls.
7. Roll each ball out into an oval shape about 1 cm thick . Poke with your fingers over the top to create little valleys, then brush with the glaze and sprinkle with sesame seeds.
8. Place on floured oven trays and leave to rise in a warm place (about 30 minutes).
9. Preheat the oven to 200°C (400°F).
10. Bake for 15 minutes or until golden brown.  Leave to cool before eating.

Makes a great accompaniment to the soups, hamburgers or kebabs recipes in this book.

# rice pudding
## ❧sheerid riza❧

4 cups full cream milk
½ cup short grain white rice
¼ cup sugar
¼ tsp saffron (optional)
1 tsp rosewater (optional)
Ground pistachios or almond slivers for garnish

10 mins prep
45 mins cooking
(+ overnight in fridge)

Ⓥ

Serves 4

1 srv ≈ 303 Cal / 1272 kJ

*Rice pudding is a universal favourite.*

*This is a simple and easy dish to make.*

1. If you plan to use saffron, grind the saffron with a ¼ tsp of sugar in a pestle and mortar to create a powder. Set this aside for later.
2. Add milk and the rice to a large pot and heat until it begins to boil. Reduce heat to low.
3. Keep stirring the rice and milk mixture until the rice has fully cooked and is soft. Approx. 35-40 minutes.
4. While still on the heat add the sugar (and saffron powder and rosewater if used) and mix until completely dissolved.
5. This final mixture will still look a little watery but will set in the fridge. However if you find that it has become too thick, add a little extra milk to thin it out otherwise it can become too solid when set in the fridge.
6. Pour rice pudding into 4 ramekins and leave to cool before putting in the fridge to set overnight.

Serve cold sprinkled with ground pistachios or slivers of almond.

*This is a unique version of the traditional French creme caramel recipe.*

*Orange and saffron work well together in flavouring this flan.*

# orange saffron flan

**FLAN**
400 ml (14 fl oz) full cream milk
3 eggs + 1 yolk
½ cup sugar
¼ tsp saffron
Vanilla pod (or 1 tsp vanilla essence)

**CARAMEL**
½ cup sugar
1 tsp vinegar
2 Tbsp orange marmalade

 20 mins prep 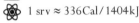 ⓥ
 30 mins baking
(+ overnight in fridge)
Serves 4
1 srv ≈ 336Cal / 1404kJ

1. Preheat oven to 155°C/310°F.

## Custard mixture
2. Grind the saffron with a teaspoon of sugar in a pestle and mortar to create a fine powder.
3. To a pot add the milk, ground saffron and vanilla. If using vanilla pod, split in half and scrape out the seeds. Add the seeds and the pod to the milk.
4. Bring just to the boil and turn off the heat.
5. In a large bowl blend the eggs and sugar until smooth. Gently pour the hot milk a little at a time over the eggs mixing quickly to combine. Set aside.

## Caramel
6. Heat the sugar with 3 Tbsp water and 1 tsp of vinegar. Allow to boil but do not mix. When it begins to darken to a caramel brown, take off the heat and quickly mix in the marmalade.

## Assemble the dish
7. Pour a few tablespoons of the caramel mixture into the base of each of the four ramekins. Leave to cool.
8. Remove the vanilla pod from the custard. Strain the custard mixture through a sieve filling each of the ramekins. Cover each ramekin with aluminium foil.

## Cooking
9. The creme caramels will be cooked in a water bath in the oven. To do this, place ramekins in a deep tray and place in the center of the oven. Using a kettle pour hot water into the tray letting it rise to half way up the ramekin's sides.
10. Cook in the oven for 25 - 30 minutes.
11. Remove from oven. Take the ramekins out of the water bath and leave to cool before transferring to the fridge to set further. The centres of the flan should be a little wobbly
12. Refrigerate for at least 4 hours (overnight is best) before serving.

To serve, run a knife around the edge of each ramekin and turn over onto a plate. The flan should pop out with the caramel sauce covering it. Serve with slivers of almond and fresh pieces of orange.

# baklava I

⏳ 20 mins prep    Ⓥ
♨ 20 mins baking
🔔 Makes: 18 pieces
⚛ 1 piece≈ 187Cal/783kJ

*Baklava is made all over the Middle East and is a popular dessert all over the world.*

*Commonly walnuts or pistachios are used as the filling, but you can also try cashews, pecans, hazelnuts or macadamia nuts.*

**BAKLAVA**
**250g (9oz) packet of filo pastry**
**150g (5.3oz) shelled pistachios**
**½ cup melted butter**

**SYRUP**
**1 cup sugar**
**1 cup water**
**10 cardamom pods**

1. Preheat oven to 180°C/350°F.

2. For the syrup, slightly crush the cardamom pods with the flat of a knife. In a small pot bring the sugar, water and cardamom to the boil. Once the sugar has dissolved, turn heat off and set aside to cool.

3. For the baklava filling, crush the pistachios in a food processor until it resembles coarse bread crumbs. Do not over process the nuts.

4. Place a whole layer of filo on a bench and brush with the melted butter. Add another layer and brush with butter again. Repeat so that there are 7 layers of filo.

5. Cut the filo into approximate 7 cm(3″) squares (ensure you divide the sheet so that there is no leftover). Add a teaspoon and a half of pistachios into the center of each square and then fold the corners into the center to resemble an envelope. Press down to close. They will open slightly when cooking. Repeat with the rest of the filo using all the filling.

6. Place on a baking parchment lined tray and cook in the oven for 15 –20 minutes or until golden.

7. Take tray out of the oven and immediately spoon a tablespoon or two of the syrup (straining out the cardamom pods) into the center of each of the baklava squares over the pistachios nuts. Leave to cool in the tray.

These are now ready to eat. Serve with freshly brewed tea or coffee.

# baklava II

**BAKLAVA**
250g (9oz) packet of filo pastry
150g (5.3oz) walnuts
½ tsp cinnamon powder
½ cup melted butter

**SYRUP**
½ cup sugar
½ cup water
½ cup honey
1 Tbsp rosewater

⏳ 20 mins prep
♨ 50 mins baking
🍲 Makes: 25 pieces
⚛ 1 piece ≈ 145 Cal/600kJ

Ⓥ

*This baklava
contains walnuts
and cinnamon
with a sweet honey
rosewater syrup.*

*The baklava is
cut in the pattern
shown below.*

1. Preheat oven to 180°C/350°F.
2. In a food processor, quickly crush the walnuts so that they resemble large bread crumbs (do not over process). Mix in the cinnamon.
3. Brush the base of a tray approx 20 x 30 cm (8 x 12″) with melted butter. Cut the filo to match the size of the tin.
4. Place a layer of filo into the tray and brush with butter. Repeat 6 more times, brushing with melted butter between each sheet.
5. Sprinkle half of the crushed walnuts evenly over the filo.
6. Layer four more layers of filo brushing with melted butter as before.
7. Add the rest of the walnuts and layer another 7 layers of filo brushing with butter in-between. Finally brush the top of the baklava with butter.
8. Cut the baklava lengthwise in 4 cm (1½″) strips. Then cut at 45° diagonally at 4 cm (1½″) intervals. See Fig 1 on the right for the cutting pattern.
9. Bake in the preheated oven for 40 - 50 minutes until golden brown.
10. While baking, prepare the syrup by adding all the sugar, honey, water and rosewater into a small pot and bring to the boil. Ensure the sugar is fully dissolved then turn off the heat.
11. When the baklava is ready, take out of the oven and immediately pour the syrup evenly over the top. It should bubble from the heat of the pan. Leave to cool in the pan before serving.

Serve with tea or coffee.

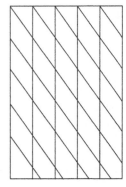

*Fig 1.*

141

# chickpea shortbread
## 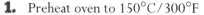naan e nokhoochi

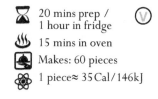
20 mins prep /
1 hour in fridge
15 mins in oven
Makes: 60 pieces
1 piece ≈ 35 Cal / 146kJ

2 cups of plain dry roasted chickpeas
½ cup of melted clarified butter
½ cup icing sugar
½ tsp ground cardamom
1 tsp rosewater
2 Tbsp roughly ground pistachios for garnish

1. Preheat oven to 150°C / 300°F
2. Place the roasted chickpeas into a food processor and blend at high speed for about 3 minutes until the peas are crushed into a fine flour.
3. Sift the chickpea flour into a mixing bowl. Discard any remnant from the sieve. You want the flour to be as fine as possible.
4. Sift in the icing sugar and ground cardamom and mix into the flour.
5. Add the rosewater and then carefully pour the clarified butter into the flour and stir through. Add a little at a time until the flour comes together to form a crumbly dough. The dough should have a golden butter-like quality.
6. Roll out into a square slab about 1 cm (approx. ½″) thick. Press in the edges if they start to crack.
7. Sprinkle the ground pistachios over the top of the slab of dough and press down gently.
8. Refrigerate for an hour.
9. Cut the slab into small 2 cm (¾ in) squares. Alternatively use a small cookie cutter. Traditionally a small clover leaf pattern is used.
10. Place shortbread on a parchment lined cookie tray and cook in the oven for 10-15 minutes until they turn pale blond. They should not brown.
11. Remove from the oven and allow to cool on the tray. Do not touch them as they will be very soft.

Once cooled, assemble on a flat dish and serve with tea or coffee.

These chickpea shortbread bites are a traditional Persian sweet and are commonly eaten during the Persian New Year.

Roasted chickpeas are fully cooked and can be eaten as snacks. They will grind well in a food processor. Use the plain variety that are not salted or flavoured.

If buying chickpea flour, always check that it is the roasted variety. Do not use raw chickpea flour for this recipe. Read the label carefully.

Note that clarified butter is simply butter that has been melted over a stove for a few minutes to let the water evaporate. The milk solids will settle to the bottom of the pot and can be easily discarded.

# pistachio ice-cream
## ❧bastani❧

🕰 10 mins prep    ⓥ
🔥 10 mins cooking
(+ freeze overnight)

🍳 Serves 4
⚛ 1 srv ≈ 597Cal/2501kJ

*If you don't have the time to make the ice-cream from scratch, buy a good quality vanilla ice-cream from the store. Allow it to soften before mixing in the rosewater and pistachios and refreeze.*

*The optional ice-cream improvers used in this recipe help to prevent the ice-cream becoming too hard after it has been frozen. Glycerin can be found in the cake baking section of the supermarket and Xanthan gum can be found in some health food or specialty stores.*

### ICE CREAM BASE
1 cup full cream milk
1 cup icing sugar
3 large egg yolks
300ml (½ pint) whipping cream

### FLAVOURING
2 Tbsp rosewater
¼ tsp saffron strands (optional)
½ cup roughly chopped pistachio

### OPTIONAL ICE CREAM IMPROVERS
2 Tbsp Glycerin
¼ tsp Xanthan gum

1. If you plan on using saffron for the flavouring, ground the saffron strands with a ¼ tsp of sugar in a pestle and mortar to create a fine powder.
2. Whip the cream into soft peaks and then set aside in the fridge.
3. Put the milk into a small pot and add the ground saffron. Bring just to the boil and then turn off the heat.
4. In another bowl blend icing sugar with yolks. Keep mixing until a thick paste is formed.
5. Slowly add the milk to the yolk mixture, stirring quickly to prevent the egg cooking.
6. Pour mixture back into the pot and return to a very low heat until it thickens (coats back of spoon). Do not boil. Approx 6 - 8 mins. Take off the heat.
7. Add the rosewater, and any of the optional ice cream improvers and mix through. Leave to cool to room temp. Once cooled, use a hand blender to blend the ingredients. This will remove any lumps from the Xanthan gum. Chill in the fridge.
8. After the custard has chilled, fold in the whipped cream.
9. Pour this into an ice-cream maker (following the ice-cream makers instructions). When the ice cream has thickened, add the chopped pistachios and mix in.
10. Spoon into an airtight container and freeze for a few hours or overnight.
11. If you don't have an ice-cream maker, freeze the mixture for an hour and then hand mix through the pistachios and place back in the freezer.

To serve, put two scoops in each persons bowl and drizzle some double cream (not whipped). This will solidify and add some extra crunch to the dessert.

# cherry or strawberry preserve

1 kg (2.2 lb) of fresh cherries (pitted)
    or strawberries
750g (1.7 lb) sugar

 20 mins+overnight (V)

 30 mins

Makes: about 3 cups

1 Tbsp ≈ 58 Cal / 241 kJ

*You can also use this method for other fruits like apricots, peaches and plums.*

*Preserves are usually served with tea as an alternative to using sugar. Put some preserve in your mouth and then sip your tea.*

## Prepare fruit

1. Add the fruit to a large bowl. If using strawberries, hull and pierce with a fork. If the strawberries are large, slice in half. For the cherries, ensure that all have been pitted.
2. Pour the sugar over the fruit and mix gently to coat.
3. Leave overnight.

## Cooking

4. The fruit should have released plenty of liquid. Transfer the fruit and the juice to a large pot and gently heat.
5. Cook for approximately 25 minutes, removing any scum that forms.
6. Occasionally stir the mixture very gently being careful not to breakup the fruit.
7. Test that the preserve is ready by tipping a few drops of the syrup in a glass of cold water and seeing that it falls to the bottom without completely dissolving in the water.
8. Do not over-cook as the syrup may begin to caramelise and the preserve will become very thick and hard when cooled.
9. Leave to cool slightly before pouring into sterile jam jars.

Preserves are traditionally served with hot tea. You can also use on hot buttered toast or scones.

# halva

1 cup vegetable oil
2 cups flour
1 cup golden syrup/honey or maple syrup
½ cup water
Walnuts or pistachios for garnish

⏳ 5 mins prep
♨ 10 mins
🍲 Makes: 35 squares
⚛ 1 piece ≈ 111 Cal/464 kJ

Ⓥ

*Unlike the familiar sesame based halva, this is made from flour.*

1. Mix the syrup with the water and set aside.
2. Heat the oil in a stainless steel pot over medium heat.
3. Add the flour to the hot oil and mix vigorously using a wooden spoon.
4. Continue mixing over medium heat ensuring that nothing sticks to the bottom of the pot. Initially, it will resemble a crumbly roux but after 5 minutes it will begin to loosen into a smooth paste. Keep mixing for a further 5 minutes.
5. Remove pot off the heat. Carefully pour the diluted syrup into the pot. It will begin bubbling and steaming. Mix rapidly until the syrup is fully incorporated and becomes a soft dough-like consistency. Mix for 2 more minutes.
6. Turn out the halva onto a flat baking tray and pat down with the back of the wooden spoon to form into a square slab about 1 cm (½″) thick.  Note it will still be very hot.
7. While still hot, cut into 2.5 cm (1″) squares. Into the middle of each square press in a piece of walnut or pistachio for garnish.

Once cooled, this is served with coffee or tea.

# turkish coffee

Turkish style coffee
sugar

⏳ 2 mins prep
♨ 4 mins on stove
🍲 1 cup per person
⚛ 1 cup ≈ 34 Cal/142 kJ

Ⓥ

*Turkish coffee is a strong coffee that is boiled over a stove.*

*A thick sediment will form at the bottom of the cup. This is not consumed.*

*Reading Turkish coffee cups (from the pattern created by the coffee sediment of an upturned cup) is an enjoyable conversation starter.*

1. In a Turkish coffee pot, add 1 heaped teaspoon of Turkish style coffee, 1 teaspoon of sugar (or ½ teaspoon if you want it less sweet) and 1 espresso cup size of cold water per person. Stir the coffee mixture.
2. Place on a medium heat. Stir occasionally and let sit.
3. Watch the coffee as it will boil over very quickly. Once it just begins to boil and a foam (crema) develops, immediately take off the heat.

Pour into the espresso cups and serve.

# brewed tea
## &chai&

*Tea is an important drink in the Assyrian culture and is drunk at any time of the day.*

*When friends come over, tea is always served along with cha-deh (roux filled pastry, page 130), noz-oo-jeh (sweet layered biscuits, page 132) and sweet preserves, page 147.*

Tea for 4 people:
3 teaspoons of a large
    loose leaf tea
1 teaspoon of an Earl
    Grey tea

Add the tea to a teapot and fill with boiling water. Allow to brew for a few minutes before straining into cups.

*In many middle eastern households, you add more tea into the teapot than necessary to create a very dark brew. Tea is strained into a cup (about a quarter of the way up) and then filled with plain boiling water to make up the desired strength.*

*Tea is usually drunk with a piece of sugar cube (ghande) in the mouth and the tea sipped through (see page 153). Sweet preserves are also used in the same manner to sweeten the tea as it is consumed (see page 147).*

# sugar cubes
## ஃghandeஃ

**500g (1 lb) granulated sugar**
**½ cup water**
**2 tsp vanilla essence (or 1 vanilla pod)**

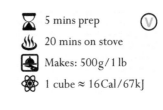

⌛ 5 mins prep
♨ 20 mins on stove
🫖 Makes: 500g / 1 lb
⚛ 1 cube ≈ 16Cal / 67kJ

Ⓥ

*When drinking tea,*
*a small piece of*
*sugar cube is placed*
*in the mouth (near*
*the cheek) and*
*the tea is sipped .*

*The sugar*
*sweetens the tea*
*as it is drunk.*

1. In a stainless steel pot add the sugar and water.
2. Mix over a medium heat and bring to the boil.
3. Keep mixing for 10 minutes.
4. Add the vanilla essence (or the seeds from the vanilla pod). Adding Vanilla may darken the sugar slightly.
5. Reduce heat and keep mixing for a further 10 minutes.
6. The mixture will remain cloudy. It should not caramelise or turn clear.
7. If the mixture dries out, add 2 Tbsp of water and continue cooking.
8. The mixture should be bubbly with sugar crystals hardening around the sides of the pot.
9. Pour onto a parchment lined baking tray and pat down with the back of a spoon to form a slab about a finger's width thickness.
10. Let cool for about 10 minutes and if it is not too hot to handle, you can begin breaking it up into small cubes.
11. Leave to cool completely and store in an airtight jar.

These vanilla sugar cubes can be used to sweeten tea or coffee.

# The pantry

**Some of the main ingredients used in these recipes**

*Onion*

*Black pepper*

*Paprika*

*Turmeric*

*Tomato paste concentrate*

*Zereshk*

*Spring Onions*

*Parsley*

### Sweet Paprika

This is the mildest of the chilli powders. It is an essential ingredient in many of the recipes in this book.

### Mild or Hot Paprika

This can be used in place of the regular sweet Paprika if you desire a bit of heat to the dish. Substitute in part or all for the recipes that use paprika.

### Turmeric

A staple spice used in Assyrian cooking.

### Ground Black pepper

Ground black pepper is used in most of the stews and is preferred over the freshly ground variety as it blends in with the other ingredients.

### Tomato paste concentrate

This is a concentrated tomato puree. It is used in many of the dishes as a base flavour.

### Parsley, coriander, dill, celery and mint

These herbs are all readily available in supermarkets and green grocers.

### Garlic Chives

You may have difficulty finding this ingredient. It is similar to spring onions, except that it has flat leaves (not tubes) and a more intense flavour. You may be able to find these in Asian groceries or your local green grocers, otherwise substitute spring onions (scallions), regular chives, or use a combination of both.

### Fenugreek leaves

This is an important ingredient in one recipe, Gormeh Zubzi (page 113). If you cannot find fresh fenugreek, you can use ground fenugreek seeds (found in the spice section of the supermarket). Grow your own by planting fenugreek seeds.

### Silverbeet

Also known as Chard, or Swiss Chard. Can be found in green grocers or supermarkets. If you cannot locate this, substitute curly kale or spinach.

### Zereshk

This is a small dried berry (barberry). It has a sweet/sour taste and is used with rice. Usually found in middle eastern grocery stores or specialty food stores. Dried cranberries are a good substitute.

### Eggplant

Also known as aubergines.

### Chickpeas

Also known as garbanzo beans.

### Basmati rice

This is a variety of long grain rice that has a fragrant aroma. A good quality Basmati rice is essential when making the rice dishes in this book. Do not substitute regular rice as you will not get the same results. Nearly all supermarkets will stock basmati rice. Try a variety of brands and stick with the one that produces the best results. Some basmati rice improves when soaked for 30 minutes before using.

*Garlic Chives*

*Fenugreek*

*Pomegranate molasses*

*Capsicum*

## Saffron

Used for its bright colour and unique aroma. This is an expensive spice and quality can vary. It can be purchased from supermarkets or specialty food stores.

## Rosewater

A fragrant water that has been infused with rose petals. It adds a unique flavour and aroma to sweet dishes. This can be found in your local supermarket or middle eastern food store.

## Pomegranate molasses

A sweet and sour syrup made from concentrated pomegranate juice. You can get it from middle eastern food stores and in some supermarkets. For the chicken recipe in this book (page 122), you can substitute pomegranate juice.

*Romano peppers*

## Onions and Garlic

Used extensively in Assyrian food.

## Romano peppers

A long sweet variety of peppers.

## Zucchini

Also known as courgettes.

## Capsicum

Also known as bell peppers.

*Saffron*

## Dried preserved lemons

Can be found in specialty food stores. Substitute the juice of a lemon in the stew if you cannot find them.

## Sumac

This is a lemony, sour, dark purple spice. Most supermarkets carry this ingredient. It is sprinkled over cooked kebabs or soaked in water to add a lemony sour flavour to cabbage dolma.

*Eggplant*

## Vine Leaves

Preserved vine leaves in brine can be found in supermarkets or specialty food stores. If you have a vine growing in the yard, you can use fresh leaves but make sure they are not sprayed with insecticide.

## Cuts of meat:
### Leg of lamb

Lamb is used in many of the recipes that require meat. The cut that is used almost exclusively is leg of lamb cut into cubes. Lamb neck fillet or lamb back strap can also be used for the casseroles.

*Leg of Lamb*

### Lamb Back strap

For lamb kebabs, a tender meat is required so lamb loin (back strap) or lamb eye fillet is used. This is a more expensive cut of meat but it is well worth it for the flavour and texture.

### Beef

While lamb is the meat most commonly used in middle eastern cooking, you can substitute beef in most of the recipes. For kebabs use a tender cut like fillet steak. For stews, use a braising steak. Also sirloin or rump steak cut into cubes works well.

*Lamb back strap*

# Index

159

# About the cook

Beatrice Youil was born in the city of
Urmia, Iran, in the village of Zatajohn, in 1937.

Beatrice and her late husband Youbert, emigrated to Australia in the late 60's and
have lived there ever since, raising a family of six children. Food has always been
an important part of Beatrice's family life. While in Australia, she has incorporated
many local recipes into her food repertoire.

In her spare time she writes Assyrian songs and poetry.  She has published a book on
her writing called "Life. Assyrian Poetry. Musings on God, love and loss."

*A pot of rice cooking on a stove with a tea
towel wrapped tightly around its lid.*

CPSIA information can be obtained at www.ICGtesting.com
Printed in the USA
LVOW022017260613

340386LV00013B/33/P

9 780957 589209